52 WEEKS
of
Esteemable Acts

of

Esteemable Acts

A Guide to Right Living

FRANCINE WARD

Hazelden
Center City, Minnesota 55012-0176

1-800-328-0094
1-651-213-4590 (Fax)
www.hazelden.org

Aside from personal experiences shared by the author, the vignettes in
this book are composites of actual situations. Any resemblance to specific
persons, living or dead, or to specific events is purely coincidental.

Library of Congress Cataloging-in-Publication Data
Ward, Francine.
    52 weeks of esteemable acts : a guide to right living /
Francine Ward.
        p. cm.
    ISBN-10: 1-59285-290-4
    ISBN-13: 978-1-59285-290-1
    1. Self-esteem. 2. Conduct of life. I. Title: Fifty two weeks of
esteemable acts. II. Title.

    BF697.5.S46W36 2005
    170'.44—dc22

                                                        2005046348

09 08 07 06 05   6 5 4 3 2 1

Cover design by David Spohn
Cover illustration by Mark Severin
Interior design by Ann Sudmeier
Typesetting by Stanton Publication Services, Inc.

Dedication

I dedicate this book to the following people:

EFFIE WARD, my grandmother, who was my rock.
She taught me that if you know how to make something,
you'll always be able to take care of yourself.
She'd be proud of what I've made of my life.

LOUISE ROBERTSON, who was relentless in her love for me
and never stopped seeing the gifts I had buried deep inside.

DR. PAUL, who saw me as an author and a communicator
long before I did.

Thank you.

Contents

Acknowledgments

It's hard to believe this is the second book in the Esteemable Acts series. It lives and breathes thanks to the support, love, guidance, inspiration, and encouragement of so many people. As always, it's hard to thank every single person who played a part in this book becoming a reality. My hope is if your name is missed, you will know that at the moment you supported me, you were already thanked a million times and that you will forever remain in my heart.

My husband, Richard, a truly giving and loving spirit, and a great dad to my cats. Thanks for being one of the good guys.

My mother, an amazing woman and someone I get to call my friend.

Carole Bidnick, my incredible agent, who has never stopped believing in me.

Becky Post, my editor, who made writing this book a really wonderful experience.

Kate Kjorlien, my fabulous manuscript editor, for being exceptionally patient with every change I made.

Peggy Byrne for being there when I needed her, for having the courage to tell me the truth, and for having me write a weekly gratitude and fear list, even when I didn't want to.

Patricia Broat, who gave me an audience and a wonderful opportunity through the Women Healing Conferences.

My friend Lorraine Friedman, who continues to show me that leaving the practice of law was not a mistake.

My friend Brenda Ferreira for being another courageous woman.

My Aunt Val and Uncle Usher for providing me with a light when I couldn't see.

The Reverend Elouise Oliver and the Reverend Andriette Earl for having the courage to tell the truth and be real from the pulpit. Your examples keep me coming back.

Wendy Merrill for her amazing editorial insight.

The Marin Sunrise Club of Rotary for being a wonderful example of service above self.

All the people who look at me and say, "If she can do it, I can do it."

All the women, men, and teenage girls who ask me for guidance and all those who use it—you are the reason I give and you are the reason I keep on giving.

The men and women who have lost their way and need guidance; those who have found their way and need a little support in taking action; those who are on the path and need a reminder to stay the course—I am here for you.

My accountability buddies who share this path with me, who keep me going when I'd rather give up: Diane Parente, Stephanie Covington, Marilee Driscoll, Lois Nightingale, Nili Sachs, Michelle Anton. To you, ladies, I say thank you.

Finally, everyone who has ever loved, inspired, motivated, supported, encouraged, or believed in me. Your love and strength carries me further than you know. Thank you.

Introduction

Hello, and welcome to the world of esteemable acts. If you picked up this book, you have not done so by mistake. You have arrived here by divine appointment.

Before moving ahead, I invite you to say the following words to yourself to get you ready for what's ahead.

> Spirit, please guide my heart as I take away what needs to be taken from this experience, and guide my hand as I write what needs to be written. There is a divine plan for my life that is now unfolding. I know that you love me just the way I am, not when I become what I perceive as perfect, but right now. I am thanking you in advance for your favor, your love, and your guidance in this moment. I am willing to do the work that lies ahead with an honest and open heart.

The "esteemable acts" approach is a fresh new way to build self-esteem, one that suggests self-esteem comes from doing esteemable acts, those things that make you feel good about yourself. Based on the concepts that led to my recovery from drug addiction, alcoholism, prostitution, low self-esteem, and codependence, esteemable acts is a courageous new path to freedom. It really works.

Over the next fifty-two weeks, you'll be invited to take actions—esteemable actions—that will move you past your limitations to a place you've never known. Along the way, you'll meet many amazing people. The most incredible person you'll meet is *you*.

Each week, you'll focus on a particular topic. There may be times when the work will appear to be more than you can handle. Do the best you can. It's your journey.

There are five basic principles of esteemable acts that will surface throughout your reading:

1. Esteemable acts do not offer a quick fix. There is work to be done. You will get fifty-two weeks of work in fifty-two weeks. And you will get out of the experience what you are willing to put into it. Over time, you will see a change.

2. Self-esteem is not the same as confidence. We mistakenly believe that if we are confident, are successful, and feel sure of ourselves, we will like who we are. This is a false assumption. While confidence may be an aspect of self-esteem, it is not the determining factor. Self-esteem comes from being in the game—making an effort—even if you feel unsure about your skills and abilities.

3. Self-esteem is not the destination. It's what happens to you along the way to living a courageous, purposeful, service-driven life. The destination is only a place; it's the journey along the way that builds character. It's what you make of your learning that defines how you feel about yourself.

4. Self-esteem comes from doing esteemable acts. You can't think your way into right living; you must act your way into right thinking. Self-esteem comes from behaving in a way that makes you feel good about yourself, which means being mindful of how you treat yourself *and* how you treat others.

5. Walking through fear is the key. Each time you overcome a challenge or complete a task you didn't think you could complete, you feel better about yourself. When you get to the other side, something magical takes place—a stronger, more empowered you is revealed.

52 Weeks of Esteemable Acts: A Guide to Right Living is a book to be studied, not just read. Perhaps you will read it alone or share the experience with others through esteemable acts groups. Whatever your choice, I hope it will become a working part of your life. The practicing of esteemable acts is an ongoing experience.

Enjoy the journey!

WEEK 1

Action Is the Key

Thought for the Week
Self-esteem comes from doing esteemable acts.

Affirmations for the Week
I am willing to do the work.

This week, I will act my way into feeling
good about me.

Esteemable Actions for the Week

DAY 1

I once had a beautiful plant. It sat on my dining-room table for three weeks as I waited for it to blossom. Each week, I waited for something to happen. By week three, instead of a luscious blooming bush, what revealed itself was a dry, shriveled piece of nothing.

I stormed angrily into the florist's shop and demanded an explanation for why my plant had died.

"You killed my plant," I shouted in a room full of customers. "You took my money and killed my plant." Now with the attention of everyone in the store, I continued to rant like a spoiled, unhappy three-year-old. "I want my money back. It's your fault. I did what you told me to do. I waited for three weeks, and now look, my plant is dead."

Puzzled, yet relatively calm, the florist asked, "Did you do everything I told you to do?"

"Absolutely! I waited for three weeks just like you said. I just waited, and now my plant is dead."

Scratching his head in wonderment, he asked, "Did you also water the plant every three days? Did you feed it the plant food I gave you? Did you keep it out of direct sunlight? Tell me, what did you do?"

"I didn't water it, because it didn't look like it needed it. I lost the food you gave me, and I didn't have time to get more. And I thought you said to keep it in direct sunlight. I waited for three weeks before calling you because I figured it would be okay. I thought if I let go and let God, the plant would eventually bloom."

He looked at me and simply said, "I'm happy to replace your plant, but your job was to take care of the plant—do the footwork *and then* let go of the results."

How easy it is to mistakenly believe that "let go and let God" means to sit back and do nothing. Our words may not speak it, but our behavior says, "If we just wait, God will provide and good things will happen without our having to do anything." *Alcoholics Anonymous,* the Big Book, teaches that faith without works is dead. To me that means that I do the work and leave the results to God.

It's no different with self-esteem. Self-esteem is not something we're born with. We don't catch it, and contrary to popular belief, we don't get it through osmosis. Instead, we get self-esteem the old-fashioned way: we earn it. We can't think our way into right living; we must act our way into right thinking. Self-esteem comes from behaving in a way that makes us feel good about ourselves, which means being mindful of how we treat ourselves *and* how we treat others. And how we treat others is as important as how we treat ourselves.

When we're disrespectful of others, it is easy to think that our behavior is an indication of power and self-esteem. On the contrary, it suggests that we care little about ourselves, because we care little about others. For years, I had many excuses for bad behavior: "I'm only human," "I'm just an alcoholic," "If you grew up like me, you'd behave the way I do." In response to my line about being an alcoholic, one of the most powerful retorts was "Alcoholism explains your behavior. It doesn't excuse your behavior." My behavior at the florist's shop was inappropriate. That was no way to speak to anyone. Eventually I went back and made amends for how I spoke to the florist. Self-esteem comes from doing esteemable acts.

This first week of *52 Weeks of Esteemable Acts* creates the groundwork for what lies ahead: actions—*esteemable actions*—designed to help you feel better about yourself. To get the most from this experience, I invite you to do the work. While at times the suggested assignments may appear difficult, they are not impossible to complete. If you need to break them down into even smaller pieces, do so. Countless people before you have ventured to change their lives through the work set forth in esteemable acts. This first day, begin thinking about your behavior. Become aware of how you treat yourself, how you allow others to treat you, and how you treat them.

DAY 2

Today is an Esteemable Health Day. The better you care for your health, the better you feel about yourself. Take the stairs every chance you get today. Make the effort. Don't let excuses stop you. Imagine how you'll feel after you've done that esteemable act for yourself. Drink three extra glasses of water, regardless of how much you normally drink. Water is a natural cleansing tonic, and it helps keep you regular.

DAY 3

Today is a day to practice acts of kindness. Sometimes we get so busy living our lives, we forget how we affect others. Today identify three situations where you could have been just a little kinder. Being mindful of how you treat others is an esteemable act.

DAY 4

Today do something nurturing for yourself that doesn't involve spending money. You get to choose. Perhaps it's taking just thirty minutes for yourself in a bubble bath, giving yourself a facial scrub, or going to the park and sitting in the sun for lunch. Perhaps you could clean your car, exercise for thirty minutes, cut flowers from your garden for your home or office, or touch base with a friend who has been there for you. You'll be amazed at how you'll feel talking to a friend you love and who loves you.

DAY 5

This is a self-worth day. Do something nice for yourself that may cost just a tiny bit of money. You get to choose. Buy some flowers if you don't have a garden, get a manicure or pedicure, or get a massage at your local massage school (where fees are low because practitioners are students). Treat yourself to something you like.

DAY 6

This is your day for letting go of your inhibitions. Do something fun today, and yes, silliness counts. Sometimes we get so focused on the doing that we forget about the fun. What one fun thing can you do today?

DAY 7

Day seven will always be the Four Rs Day, a day for you to rest, recharge, regroup, and review your week. What observations can you make about your behavior this week? What worked? What didn't? What day seemed extra hard? Why? For some of you, this day will seem less important than the previous six, because there is less to do. I urge you to practice the four Rs. We often talk about balance, but rarely are we willing to do what it takes to create it.

WEEK 2

Journaling: A Tool for Success

Thought for the Week

It's an esteemable act to have the courage to put
your thoughts on paper.

Affirmations for the Week

I think, I write, I understand.

This week, I will journal my way to good health.

Esteemable Actions for the Week

DAY 1

Twenty-five years ago, I was introduced to journaling and didn't like
it one bit. But it saved my life.

My greatest fear was that if others really knew who I was, they
wouldn't like me. Writing about my feelings was a surefire way to
reveal myself. So why would I ever do something that would enable
someone else to know me better?

Still, a friend kept encouraging me to write down my feelings. I
was told that my feelings were valid, that they wouldn't be used
against me, that I wouldn't be judged for my poor writing skills, and
that I didn't have to do it perfectly. Slowly I became willing to try
journaling. Today writing my thoughts on paper has become an important and useful part of my life. Journaling provides me with an

outlet to express my thoughts, share my feelings, and note observations. Ultimately journaling provides me with a way to capture my creative voice.

So what is journaling and why is it important? It's the act of writing our thoughts on paper in one easy-to-manage notebook called a journal. It's a tool for self-discovery. I encourage you to keep your journal handy at all times, because you never know when an important feeling or thought will surface. Our journal is a living document that we can refer to over time. It is our treasure book, filled with lessons learned, questions asked, questions answered, pictures and ideas reflected on, and the exercises done throughout our journey.

Journaling is a powerful tool for self-expression. We can be as creative as we like. Journaling gives us an opportunity to make our thoughts "real," rather than leaving them as unexpressed musings. Journaling clarifies our perspective. Sometimes just seeing our thoughts gives us new personal insights. Once we've identified our feelings, the next step is to get past some of them. Journaling helps us do that. Through writing, we move into the solution by capturing important thoughts that otherwise might disappear. Oftentimes great ideas die a quick death because they never see the light of day.

Finally, journaling adds "texture," or deeper dimension, to our ideas. One of my favorite classes in law school was constitutional law because it made history come alive. It added texture to historical facts. It not only made the events real but also made them interesting.

You may resist journaling because you think you have nothing to say. No need to fret; many of us feel that way. All I ask you to do is make a good-faith effort. Start somewhere. This week, you'll be given several opportunities to journal. These guided opportunities will help you write about things that you know about, feel, or are experiencing. The very act of writing is cathartic and nourishing for the soul because we release concerns that keep us emotionally blocked.

There is something magical about putting pen to paper and unlocking experiences that, in some cases, we've buried for years. Releasing our thoughts is often the scariest idea of all. Yet I have discovered that when left inside me, my feelings become even more frightening because there is no way to check them against reality. I play the same negative tape over and over, never giving myself a chance for a reality check.

Journaling is not about being smart, being artistic, or even making sense. It's about putting our thoughts onto paper. It's about writing. No one will read what you write except you, so don't worry about editing your thoughts or your grammar. Journaling is a tool that enhances our emotional growth or recovery.

DAY 2

This is the Go Get Your Journal Day. You probably have dozens of empty journals or notebooks lying around the house. Any size will do, as long as it has a lot of pages. Get one, dust it off, and make it personal. It's your special book, reflective of who you are. Color in it, paste pictures in it, and write all over it. This is your esteemable acts journal. It is one of the most important tools you'll use during the next fifty-two weeks.

DAY 3

It's time to practice journaling. At the top of the first page, write "Practice Journal Session 1." Now, about three or four lines from the top, start writing about how you feel at this very moment. It could be about the assignment I've given you—maybe you think it's a great idea and maybe you don't. It could be about some experience you just had or about your feelings in this moment. Whatever your thoughts, write about them.

DAY 4

At the top of the next page of your esteemable acts journal, write "Practice Journal Session 2." As you go through this day, focus on what people or animals are doing. For example, spend two minutes focusing on two people talking in an animated way, a dog playing in the park, a cat resting, a child being a child. Then write about your experience watching them do whatever they are doing.

DAY 5

For "Practice Journal Session 3," write about your greatest personal achievement. Something you've done that you're proud of. Maybe you lost a significant amount of weight, maybe you went back to school and got a degree, maybe you helped a friend through a rough period, or maybe you finished a race. How did you feel when it was happening? How do you feel about the experience now? Whatever it is, journal about it today.

DAY 6

For "Practice Journal Session 4," write about your best friend. Capture on paper your thoughts and feelings about this person and why he or she is important to you. And yes, it's okay if your best friend is your pet. So go ahead; get busy journaling.

DAY 7

This is your Four Rs Day, the day where you rest, recharge, regroup, and review your week. What observations can you make about this week's experience, about your willingness to journal? What worked? What didn't work? What day seemed extra hard? Why? You already know you'll feel better when you make the four Rs an active part of your week. Now that you've gotten started, enjoy the process of putting pen to paper each week. Happy journaling!

Week 3

Live Your Life on Purpose

Thought for the Week

Self-esteem comes from having the courage
to live a purposeful life.

Affirmations for the Week

I deserve to live a purposeful life.

This week, I will take action to discover
my true purpose.

Esteemable Actions for the Week

DAY 1

Recently, a woman came to me for help in defining her life's purpose.

"I'm forty-three years old," she said, "and I haven't a clue what I want to do with the rest of my life."

"What are you passionate about?" I asked. "What makes your heart sing and your spirit sparkle?"

"I'm not sure," she said. "I see other people happy, doing what seems to make them feel fulfilled. They seem so clear about what they were called to do with their lives. But me, I just don't get it. What's wrong with me?"

"Nothing," I said. "You are exactly where you're supposed to be at this moment in time, and this moment will change before you know it."

We are all on a path that's specific to each of us. Our experiences, at the moment we have them, are uniquely ours. Some people discover their true place in life at an early age. I recall knowing a few teenagers and young adults over the years who knew their purpose early on. They knew that joining the Peace Corps or VISTA, or even being a veterinarian, was their calling. Then I've known grown people who have never truly known what they are called to do. Some discover their purpose after a traumatic and painful experience, such as recovering from an illness, the loss of a loved one, a divorce, or an accident. Then still others, like me, must walk a few additional miles in life before knowing their true purpose. Whatever our path, knowing our purpose comes with responsibility—the responsibility to do the work to make it a reality and help others along the way.

It's not easy to know our destiny, our life's work, our personal mission. There are obstacles along the way, not the least of which is fear, our most powerful and debilitating opponent. It weakens our spirit and saps us of the will to move forward. Fear can then compel us to make excuses for inaction. Its mission—if we allow it—is to keep us stuck and unconscious. Sometimes the voice of fear sounds rational, convincing us that we are only one person, and one person can't make a difference. Fear tells us our voice doesn't matter, our one vote doesn't count, and our seemingly small contribution to the world is insignificant. Furthermore, fear reminds us that our plate is already full.

So how do we get past the obstacles in order to find our true purpose in life? How do we quiet that voice that says, "Don't bother"? What steps can we take to gain clarity? Following are a few questions designed to get you thinking about your reason for being. You're invited to go to that place deep within, the place where your heart longs to live a purposeful life, a life rich in meaning. By the end of this week, if you have done the work suggested, you will have a clearer idea as to your purpose. You will have the beginning of a personal mission statement.

DAY 2

Today consider your passion in life. In your esteemable acts journal, write down what you are passionate about. What gets your juices flowing? What excites you? What angers you? Are there social injustices you'd change if you could? Are there causes you'd die for? Perhaps you care deeply about homelessness, at-risk children, battered women, alcoholism, drug addiction, or illiteracy. Maybe it's the environment, your religious or spiritual beliefs, the protection of animals, or the political leadership of our country. Whatever it is, today is your day to come clean. What moves you to act?

DAY 3

Intricately tied to your purpose in life are the things you value. Again, grab your esteemable acts journal and spend today identifying your personal values. What principles guide your life? For example, a few of mine are courage, accountability, baby steps, personal growth, integrity, service, family and friends, and education. What do you value? What's important in your life? Then, next to each word or phrase, write a sentence describing why it is important to you.

DAY 4

Today let's look at how your values show up in the world. How do you manifest your values? For example, if you value health, you eat properly, exercise your body regularly, and practice mindfulness as to how you treat your body. If you value personal growth, you are probably taking classes, reading inspirational and self-help material, and being open to feedback. If you value family and friends, you make time for them. How do you demonstrate your personal values? Make some notes in your esteemable acts journal.

DAY 5

Today your focus is on what you have to give. What challenges have you overcome in life? Perhaps you overcame an addiction or dealt with a family member with an addiction. Perhaps you were abused or were an abuser. Maybe you battled dyslexia or mental illness and had to fight your way back—and did. Maybe you struggled against odds to get to where you are. Might you be interested in helping others overcome a similar challenge? What group of people would you help if you could? What could you offer them?

DAY 6

By now your juices should be flowing. You should be thinking about what touches your soul at a deep level. What do you perceive—at this time—as your life's work? What are you called to do? Today you're invited to create a draft of your personal mission statement in your esteemable acts journal. Here are some examples of what your mission statement might look like:

- My life's mission is to use my skills and talents to improve my community.
- My mission in life is to raise my family in a way that reflects my spiritual life.
- My personal mission is to educate, inspire, and empower women and girls to build their self-esteem by acquiring the tools to make appropriate choices.
- My mission is to eradicate illiteracy—one person at a time.

DAY 7

Day 7 is the Four Rs Day, a day for you to rest, recharge, regroup, and review your week. What observations can you make about your behavior this week? Do you have an emerging sense of purpose? What exercises worked? What exercises didn't work? What day seemed extra hard? Why? Are you closer to knowing your life's purpose?

Mentors Are a Gift from God

Thought for the Week

It's an esteemable act to say yes to people
who are willing to help.

Affirmations for the Week

I am open to meeting my mentor.

This week, I will meet my mentor.

Esteemable Actions for the Week

DAY 1

Almost every time I give a talk and share my story, I'm asked, "Was there one person who helped you most along the way?" It's a good question because for years I believed that everything I accomplished I did alone. Today I know that's not true.

When our lives are going well, we don't often stop to think about how we got to where we are. We are oblivious to the countless individuals who have helped us—in big and little ways. Yet without their assistance, most of us wouldn't have survived.

I was blessed with mentors long before I recognized them as such. There have always been people who have helped me along the way, including Ms. June, my elementary school day-camp counselor; Myra Goldstein, my third grade teacher; and Louise

Robertson, the first woman who had the courage to call me on my bad behavior.

So what's a mentor? Someone who's walked the path before us. And because they've been where we want to go, they often possess skills, talents, insights, and experiences we lack. Like a favored teacher, a wonderful life coach, or a special therapist, a mentor cares about our success. He or she is willing to help us reach both our professional and personal goals. Unlike a teacher, life coach, or therapist, mentors sometimes don't get paid. They just do it for the love of the game. They possess the time, energy, and inclination to help us at different stages of our journey. Regardless of whether they're paid, mentors play an integral role in our lives.

Why are they important? Because sometimes we need an example, someone with the courage to push us and tell us the truth. Louise Robertson was that person for me. She was the first person— whom I'd listen to—who had the courage to tell me how inappropriate my behavior was. And I didn't like it one bit. She was the first to tell me that self-esteem comes from doing esteemable acts, and that if I acted like a whore, I'd be treated like one.

"If you dress like a hooker," she'd say, "you're going to be treated like one. And if every word out of your mouth is a four-letter word, don't be surprised with the response you get from people."

I resented her because I believed she didn't understand me. But in truth, she understood me just fine. Today so much of who I am as a woman is due to her being who she was, her truth-telling, and her courage to be there for me, even when I was incapable of being there for myself.

Why is mentoring so important? It allows us to pass on what has been given to us to those who really want to learn. It gives us an opportunity to be of service in a very specific way.

So how do you find a mentor? In many cases, they are already in your life. They may even be a teacher or a coach. The first thing to do is identify why you want a mentor. What specific area of your life needs improving? Perhaps you're new on the job and want to learn the ropes. Maybe you want to start a business or grow an existing one. Maybe you want to learn a new skill or become more proficient at one you already have. You can have more than one mentor, so be specific about what you want. Whatever it is, make sure it's a condition you're serious about changing or improving.

Next make a short list of people who have the skills that you want and/or who have accomplished what you want to accomplish. Identify the characteristics of your ideal mentor. You want someone who has exceptional skills at reaching a goal, despite the obstacles. It could be someone working in your department, in your organization, or in your industry. It could be a local leader in your community or someone you heard speak. It could even be a relative. The key is to find someone with a proven track record of success in the area in which you need improvement.

Finding the right mentor is one thing, but being the right mentee is quite another. In determining whether you are able to be mentored, here are a few questions to ask yourself:

- Are you teachable? Do you think you have all the answers? If you believe you can't learn from others, a mentor at this time in your life isn't for you. Being teachable is the first step to being open to mentoring. Once you get that, you are well on the road to success.
- Are you able to ask for help? It's not always easy, yet it's an essential ingredient in being mentored. Sometimes the ideal mentor will approach you, but in most cases, you'll have to do the work, starting with asking for help. On the other hand, maybe you know you need help, but you're afraid to ask for it. Fear, pride, ego, laziness, anger, and resentment all get in the way of asking for help. Not allowing those things to interfere with your journey is crucial.
- Are you willing to use what you learn? Don't waste a mentor's time. Don't expect your mentor to continually share valuable time, energy, and resources with you if you're not willing to put his or her advice into practice. If you don't want the advice, don't ask for it.

- Do you take the time to appreciate people who have done nice, thoughtful things for you? Saying thank you is a simple yet often forgotten gesture. Don't take for granted the time and efforts of other people. No one has to do anything for you. Remember to say thank you often.
- Are you good at keeping appointments? Most mentors are busy and have chosen to take time out of their day to help you. It's important that you show up, and if you can't, be sure to cancel in advance.

Finally, you need a plan of action for approaching your mentor. What will it take to get that person on your team? Maybe he or she already is and you just don't know it. This week, you're invited to seek out a mentor and make yourself ready for the experience.

DAY 2

Today is your day for identifying your purpose for wanting a mentor. Why does such a relationship appeal to you? What in your life could use improvement? Are you ready for a change? Are you ready to do the work? What will you bring to the table? Write out your purpose for wanting a mentor.

DAY 3

This is your day to identify your ideal mentor. What traits would you like him or her to have? This will likely depend on your purpose. For example, if you want to be promoted in your job, you'll likely consider someone who is assertive, self-motivated, persistent, and courageous.

DAY 4

Today you get to make a short list of potential candidates. On paper, write the names of three to six people who have the skills and experiences you want and who have accomplished what you want to accomplish. List people you admire. Remember, this is just a list. Don't let your fear stop you. Next reduce your list to two or three people who could reasonably be a mentor.

DAY 5

Today get busy making phone calls, sending e-mails, or writing letters to those on your short list. Keep in mind that some people will not be able to accept your invitation because they are too busy or are already working with other mentees. Or perhaps being a mentor poses a conflict for them. Regardless, don't be discouraged. If they politely say, "No, thank you," you say, "Thank you for your time" and go to the next name on the list.

DAY 6

Don't give up. You may not find your mentor today or even next month, but if you create an intention to be mentored, are willing to do the work, and are patient, you will find the right person. Today you will network and reach out to people who might know someone you can ask.

DAY 7

Day 7 is the Four Rs Day, a day for you to rest, recharge, regroup, and review your week. What observations can you make about your actions this week? What worked? What didn't work? What day seemed extra hard? Why?

WEEK 5

Forgiveness: The Gift You Give to You

Thought for the Week

It's an esteemable act to forgive.

Affirmations for the Week

I release and forgive.

This week, I choose not to go into the future
with unresolved resentments.

Esteemable Actions for the Week

DAY 1

Paul and I hadn't spoken to one another in more than two years. And not a day passed without my wishing it were otherwise. Whenever his name was mentioned in conversation, an uneasy feeling washed over me. In the early days of our not talking, that feeling would surface as anger and resentment against him: "Who does he think he is? I can't stand him. He hurt me." I'd play those old angry tapes over and over in my mind, totally allowing him to live rent free in my brain. Yet still, my thoughts would sometimes change to "I wonder how he's doing. He's getting on in years. And to think we had been so close for so long."

Paul had been one of the single most important people in my

life, and for more than two years, that closeness turned to bitterness. The meals shared, the phone calls exchanged, the times spent with him, his wife, and their two dogs in Laguna Niguel were but distant memories.

It's amazing how small misunderstandings can turn into big conflicts, especially when we feel we're right. And it was that sense of being right that not only kept me separated from my friend and mentor for too many years but also made me unable to see any part I had played in the events that unfolded. All I knew was that I was right and he was wrong. I waited patiently for him to get that and apologize to me. He never did. And the truth is, whether my part was small or large, it didn't matter. As long as I carried a grudge, as long as I held on to my deep-seated resentment, the outcome remained the same: we were estranged.

Then something happened. A moment of sanity set in. I'm not sure why on that particular day I was willing to do what I hadn't been willing to do in the past, but I was. Perhaps it was the strong words I heard from someone I admired and trusted: "Francine, you can either be right or comfortable. Stop letting your ego control your life. Don't allow your pride to make a decision you'll regret for the rest of your life."

"But you don't understand," I cried. "He hurt my feelings. I relied on him."

Making amends, offering or accepting forgiveness, seeing our part in a conflict are all intricately connected to one another. It's hard to truly make amends for a wrong we've done or forgive someone else for a wrong they've done unless we're able to see the part we played in creating the experience.

Eventually I was able to see my part with the help of someone who loved me enough to tell me the truth. When Paul died in 2000, we were friends again. We had been reconnected for almost two years. I was grateful to have known this incredible man, this incredible spirit, but I was most grateful that I had had the courage to resolve the issue before it was too late.

It's easy to think that there will always be time to clean up the mess, that we can do it later. Yet sometimes we wait until it's too late. Contrary to the belief of many, when people die, we can never really be forgiven or forgive. We can say the words or repeat affirmations, but in truth, once people are gone, they are gone. And any unresolved issues will live on with us. So as a result of this experience, I've become an advocate for cleaning up the unresolved issues now: not putting them off until tomorrow, but addressing them today.

Is there someone against whom you carry a grudge? Are there unresolved relationship issues in your life? Are there people whom you can't seem to forgive or don't want to? While there are countless authors who say it's okay not to forgive, I am a voice with a different perspective. We may no longer care about the other person, but to allow ourselves to live with that toxicity—and make no mistake about it, anger is toxic—we suffer, our kids suffer, everyone around us suffers.

This week, you're invited to do the right thing for your peace of mind. As always, take small, conscious, consistent, baby steps to accomplish what you want. The key is to be willing, really willing, to do something.

DAY 2

Think about someone you're angry with, regardless of the reason. Try to recall a time when you were friends, before the anger set in. What was it like? How did you feel? Who else is in this category? If you're honest, there may be more people than you think. For years, my mother was at the top of my "I hate you" list. And I had no idea of the power my hatred had on every other relationship in my life. Today my mom is one of my closest friends. It took work—a lot of work—and many baby steps. Who is on your list?

DAY 3

Today is your day of prayer. Do some prayer work around creating an *intention to forgive*. The key to forgiving is being willing to forgive—not just giving it lip service—but really being willing to forgive from your heart up to your head. An intention is nothing more than a genuine willingness to make something happen. Yet willingness without action is fantasy. Getting to the place of genuinely forgiving Paul was a challenge for me because I felt so wronged by him. Yet until I was *willing* to forgive, I couldn't forgive. Praying to be willing is the first step in recovery from deeply rooted resentments.

DAY 4

Today I encourage you to find someone with whom you can share your feelings. While it's easy to find people to support you in holding on to the anger, I invite you to be courageous and seek out someone who can and will support you in forgiving. Forgiveness work is done more for you than for the person you're forgiving.

DAY 5

Spend today thinking about your reasons for holding on to your anger. Look at your fears. Perhaps you fear what people will think, or you fear that forgiveness means acceptance of the past behavior. Perhaps you fear that you will have to befriend this person if you forgive him or her. Sometimes it helps to look at the "payoff." What payoff, or benefit, do you get from holding on to the grudge? And trust me, there is always a payoff, always a reason that keeps us doing whatever it is we do. Write out your answers in your esteemable acts journal.

DAY 6

As hard as it is to really get past anger to forgiveness, you must examine your own behavior to see whether there was a part you played. And ask yourself the question, "Did I contribute to this conflict?" In some cases, you bear no responsibility. For example, a child never asks to be molested nor does a woman ask to be raped or beaten. However, there are times when your behavior contributes to the outcome. I recall a time when I was fired from a job. While I didn't ask to be fired, my work was not up to the standards of the company and I complained all the time about how I hated my job. Were they wrong to get rid of me?

DAY 7

You're at day 7 again. Your day to rest, recharge, regroup, and review your week. What observations can you make about your willingness to forgive? Was the idea of addressing unresolved issues challenging? What worked? What didn't work? What day seemed extra hard? Why?

WEEK 6

One Baby Step at a Time

Thought for the Week

Self-esteem comes from taking action—
one baby step at a time.

Affirmations for the Week

I am willing to take small, consistent,
daily action.

This week, I will baby step my way to success.

Esteemable Actions for the Week

DAY 1

I couldn't believe my eyes. One day the gravel inside our fish tank was pressed flat as if leveled by a steamroller. The following morning, there was a mountain sloping along the left side of the tank, almost reaching the top.

I wondered what happened, but assumed my husband had reconfigured the tank for some reason. Who else could have done it?

"Richard," I said, "did you rearrange the fish-tank gravel for a particular reason?" I waited for a reasonable response.

"No, Cine," he said. "I didn't do it. Ben did it."

"Ben?" I laughed. "Yeah, right. Don't be silly, Richard, Ben's a fish." He was an extraordinarily beautiful black-and-white, horizontally striped Engineer Goby. For years, he was half of the dynamic duo of Ben and Jerry, and the oldest fish in our tank. When I arrived in Marin County eight years ago, he was here. He's still around.

"Stop making up a story," I said. The fish didn't create that big mountain, especially not overnight.

"Francine," he said, "I really didn't do it. The other day, I saw Ben pick up a mouthful of gravel, swim a few inches, then spit it out."

I said, "But look at how big that mountain is. How could he have done that all by himself? He's a fish."

A few days later, I caught Ben in the act. I watched in amazement as this thin eel-like fish, with a tiny opening for a mouth, created a foothill for a mountain larger than himself. What a remarkable demonstration of an esteemable act. Through small, conscious, consistent actions, he accomplished his goal.

This reminds me of the story of the tortoise and the hare. The hare is slick and quick but never makes it to the finish line. The tortoise is the perceived loser. No one thinks he'll even make it to the finish line, let alone win the race. Yet he does. Why? Because he never gets cocky, doesn't give up, and takes small, conscious, baby steps toward the finish line. I am the tortoise. And I continue to baby step my way to success.

How easy it is to think accomplishing our goals depends on taking huge leaps in record speed. In truth, most of us get to the finish line by taking small, conscious steps—one step at a time. For the goby, one small pebble at a time grew into a mountain. For the tortoise, one small step at a time got him to the finish line.

It works! Consciously doing something over and over again works. But regardless of how well it works and how great the rewards, baby steps are a concept that's hard to grasp. Why? We live in a society that judges people by the big steps they take. We give credit for reaching the destination, not for the journey along the way. Not only do we not encourage the taking of small steps, we penalize people for taking too long to get to a destination.

Furthermore, taking baby steps is tedious work and is often perceived as hard. And most of us simply don't want to work that hard. We want the results, but we don't want to do what it takes to get there. We start a project, stop, start again, and then want to rest. It's hard to stay focused on the task at hand—even if it's something we say we want.

Another thing that gets in our way is the need to do everything yesterday. Almost without exception, my clients come to me in need of motivation. They've spent months and, in some cases, years doing nothing. Then, all of a sudden, they are inspired to take action. The problem is they then want to do everything *yesterday*. They don't want to wait or do a little at a time. Instead they want to do it all at once; they want to make up for lost time. The idea of baby steps is repulsive to them and gets tossed out of the window. Yet, as in Alcoholics Anonymous or any Twelve Step program, doing something a day at a time leads to success.

The greatest benefit of baby steps is getting the job done. Because we have been consistently doing something, it is completed in a shorter amount of time than we could imagine. Furthermore, we feel good about ourselves because we stayed the course. We kept our agreement with ourselves.

How do we get beyond our aversion to taking one small step at a time? We take action. We become willing to consistently do what we often perceive as the work. Here are a few actions that helped me shift my thinking from destination focused to baby-step focused:

- Create an intention to honor your healing journey, every step of the way. Progress is rarely made by leaps and bounds, but by consistent, small action steps.

- Start being your own biggest fan. If you don't appreciate your small steps, how can you expect others to?
- Break tasks into small pieces. See each action item as a mini-goal. It makes your tasks mentally and emotionally manageable.
- Remind yourself that every action counts. Repeat to yourself, "Every action I take moves me closer to my overall goal."
- Pray for support, and then use it.

This week, you're invited to work on the small actions, to focus on the baby steps that will get you where you want to be.

DAY 2

Identify a task or a goal you've avoided because it seems too big to handle. Perhaps it's training for a 5-mile race or a 26.2-mile marathon. Maybe it's building your new dream house, planning your family vacation or your wedding, studying for a test, or starting a new business. Maybe it's simply cleaning out the attic that you've long avoided, starting that exercise plan you've talked about, writing that book, or saving for a new car. Today is your day to get clear and honest. Write down the task.

DAY 3

What gets in the way of your taking action? For the most part, it's some form of fear. Today identify the fear you believe is blocking your progress on this task. For example, is it fear of success and what kind of responsibility that might bring? Fear of failure, fear of making a mistake, fear of not being able to sustain the momentum? These are only a few. Think of your own.

DAY 4

This is your day to do something. Take one small action. Like the goby, pick up one mouthful of gravel at a time and move it a little closer to where you want it to be.

DAY 5

Identify someone who can encourage you to take baby steps and stay the course when it gets hard. That someone could be your therapist, a parent, a spouse or companion, a life coach, or just a supportive group of like-minded friends. Whoever it is, ask for and use their help.

DAY 6

Today you get to pick up more gravel. What is another small action you can take toward reaching your goal?

DAY 7

For some of you, this was a tough week because it was about developing a new way of thinking. Bravo for having the courage to do it! Now on this seventh day, you rest, recharge, regroup, and review your week. What observations can you make about your willingness to take baby steps? What worked? What didn't work? What day seemed extra hard? Why?

WEEK 7

Courage to Dream

Thought for the Week

Self-esteem comes from having the courage
to dream.

Affirmations for the Week

I am willing to stretch beyond my comfort zone.

This week, I walk through my fear
and identify my heart's desire.

Esteemable Actions for the Week

DAY 1

Are you living the life you really want to live? Are you doing what makes your heart sing and your spirit sparkle? Do you wake up most mornings feeling blessed that you get to do what you love? If your answer is a resounding yes, then bravo, for you are among those who shine their light ever so brightly and create a path for others. You show, by example, how to live life fully and on purpose. And if you are not yet there, I invite you to take a risk this week—and indeed a risk it is. For it takes great courage to dream.

You may be thinking, "It doesn't take courage to dream." And no doubt for some of you that's true. Perhaps you grew up in a family where you were told that you could have whatever you wanted, that the sky was the limit simply because of who you are. Or perhaps you were taught you could have *almost* anything you wanted. While the moon may have been out of reach, the top of the fence was not. You simply had to set your mind to it and it would be yours.

The vast majority of you, I suspect, were discouraged from dreaming, from finding your passion. "You can't do it." "You'll never make it, so why even try?" "You're too old." "You're too young." "You're not smart enough." "Why don't you get a real job?" "We need you at home to help with the family." "What a silly idea." These may have been the words you heard most often. If you're female, perhaps you grew up in a family where the boys ruled and you were only encouraged to get married and have kids. Maybe if you took an interest in sports or science or math, you were encouraged to consider economics instead. Or maybe you wanted to be a singer, a dancer, or a musician, and you were told you should get a real job. Whatever you were told, it affected you greatly, so much so that even today the voices of those who said you couldn't still ring loud and clear in your mind.

This week, you're invited to go on a journey, a courageous journey, one that can possibly change the course of your life forever. My hope is that by your willingness to take one small step, you will be motivated to take yet another, and another, leading eventually to a life you really want.

It took me years to change the belief system that consistently said, "You can't," "You'll never make it," and "Who do you think you are?" I had to be willing to feel the uncomfortable feelings that surfaced every time I talked about being a lawyer. I had to say, "Thank you for sharing" to all those people I perceived as dream busters. I had to stop giving them power.

The year was 1981, and I was fast approaching the completion of my second year of sobriety. Something was missing. I couldn't put my finger on it, but I knew there was something unsettling about my life. I was unhappy and unsure why. There was a void inside of me, a hole in my gut, one that had always been temporarily filled with drugs, alcohol, and men. Yet for the first time in my life, I knew the emptiness could only be satisfied by something from within. I yearned to know that my life had meaning, that it was about more than just not drinking. Don't get me wrong, I was grateful to be sober, grateful not to be killing myself with drugs and alcohol. But I needed to know that I could take the lessons I learned in recovery into the real world and live a useful and happy life. I needed to know it was okay to dream of a better life.

Finding myself at that crossroad, I saw my life with a clarity I'd never known before. It was time to get real. It was time to get honest. It was time to change. And I was ready. It was a change that compelled me to ask some tough questions, such as what do I want to do with the rest of my life? What am I willing to do to make it happen?

I started by asking questions of people who seemed to be living the life they wanted. I audited classes at the local university and made friends with the reference librarian at my local library. I looked at magazines that appealed to me and then cut out pictures of things that seemed especially interesting. I read books that helped me identify my skills, talents, and things I enjoyed doing, but most often, I prayed to be an open channel. I prayed to know my life's purpose.

Why is identifying our heart's desire so important to our self-esteem? Dreams are what life is made of; they give us a reason to get out of bed in the morning and a reason to keep going, especially on those days we want to give up. When we live our lives on purpose, everyone benefits, because when we're happy, people around us are happy. When we hate the lives we have, consciously or unconsciously, we make everyone suffer. There is a power in loving what we do. There is also a sense of destructiveness when we don't. Being stuck in a job we hate or a relationship that is unhealthy debilitates the soul.

So what do you want to do when you grow up? If you could do anything in the world you want, go anyplace, experience anything, what would it be? Now is the time to take that first courageous step into the light.

The first leg of your incredible journey into real and lasting self-esteem is to tap into your heart's desire. This week, you're invited to identify what you would do with your life if you could. If you're lucky enough to already know what you want, this week of exercises will help you commit to next steps.

Armed with your creative thinking cap and a courageous spirit, you're invited to think about your dreams this week. On this first day, just allow your mind to wander. Don't write anything down. Just begin to imagine the impossible. Allow yourself to enter the field of unlimited possibilities.

DAY 2

With no particular order in mind, start writing. List fifteen things you would do with your life if you could. Consider places you'd visit, activities you'd participate in, experiences you'd have, people you'd meet, unfinished business you'd clean up. Snap your fingers and just imagine—you're there.

Picture for a moment that anything is possible. Imagine that whatever you need to make the dream real will be available. What would you be doing? Perhaps you'd get your high school diploma or an advanced degree. Maybe you'd become a doctor, accountant, or forensic scientist, or maybe you'd go to law school or start your own business. Maybe your dream would be to get out of debt, buy a house, lose weight, or let go of an addiction. Whatever the dream, allow yourself the opportunity to think about it. This week, you have permission to dream. Don't worry about making it happen, just dream. This is your week for dreaming. Start writing!

DAY 3

Right about now, you may be feeling a little discouraged, disappointed in your progress, or stuck and unable to come up with even one dream. Wherever you are in the process, stop and congratulate yourself. Coming up with one dream—let alone fifteen—is a difficult task. So wherever you are, I celebrate you. Keep up the good work. You can do it. Do the best you can.

DAY 4

Continue the process of identifying your dreams. Use this day to expand on the details. Flesh out your dreams with more specifics of how you'd like them to unfold. By this day, the "committee" in your brain will really start to chatter, trying to sabotage your success. Don't let it. You simply say, "Thank you for sharing" and keep on doing the footwork.

DAY 5

Your list should be pretty complete by now. Review it. Make sure everything you want is on it. Now reduce the list to your top ten dreams, then your top five, then your top three, and finally your number-one dream.

DAY 6

Let's convert your top dream to a SWARM goal:

S = specific
W = written
A = achievable
R = realistic
M = measurable

This is the process of converting your dream to something specific and measurable. For example, suppose your dream is to get your high school diploma during the next few years. This is how it would look in SWARM format:

S = I want to get my high school diploma by June 30, 2007.

W = I will make sure I have my goal written down in places where I can see it as a visual reminder, such as on colored index cards at work, at home, and in my car.

A = Getting a high school diploma is an achievable goal.

R = Getting a high school diploma in two years is realistic if I have time to complete the necessary work and I don't have other commitments that would get in my way. For example, it would be unrealistic if I dropped out of school in the sixth grade and had a lot of work to make up, plus I'm a single parent with a full-time job. Not that it couldn't be done—I'd just be creating more of a challenge for myself. It might be more realistic to extend the date to June 30, 2008.

M = I will establish a time by when I will have realized my goal. By June 30, 2007, I'll know whether I have a high school diploma or not.

That's it for the week. As always, esteemable acts are about taking one baby step at a time. So do the best you can.

DAY 7

This is your Four Rs Day, the day when you rest, recharge, regroup, and review your week. What observations can you make about your dreams? What worked for you this week? What didn't? What day seemed extra hard? Why? You are now ready to move on to week 8.

Week 8

Keep Your Eye on the Goal

Thought for the Week

Self-esteem comes from staying focused
on your goal.

Affirmations for the Week

I am focused on the task at hand.
This week, I will follow through on all
assignments I start.

Esteemable Actions for the Week

DAY 1

Outside our bedroom window is a hummingbird feeder. Each day one, two, and sometimes three birds at a time come and partake in the prepared meal of red sugar water. On this day, I was particularly fascinated by their swift-moving little bodies. One after another, the hummingbirds zipped up to the feeder and, with careful precision, aimed and fired their beaks into the tiny holes. And each and every time they reached their target.

How did they do it without smashing their little beaks into the side of the bird feeder, I wondered? It seemed that at least once, they'd miss the mark. But they never did. After watching them intently for about twenty minutes, I realized they got their beaks into

43

the hole every time because they were focused. They are clear about their goal: to get food. They know how to make that happen: get their beaks into the holes of the hummingbird feeder. They know what it takes: being focused—and they are—every time.

Focus is the key to making something happen. It's about being attentive to the goal, about keeping the end in mind. I learned from a wise person, many years ago, that where I place my attention is what I manifest.

Bring to mind your own experience. How many times have you attempted to complete a task or satisfy a need, and someone else's wishes took priority? How many times have you made a commitment to yourself and not kept it? How many times have you just allowed stuff to get in the way of your doing what you said you'd do? Once in a while, perhaps, it's not a problem; it's part of human nature. But when regularly neglecting our needs and desires becomes a lifestyle choice, we pay dearly. And with each mental detour, the price gets higher as our self-esteem sinks.

So why do we get off track? Why do we allow ourselves to lose sight of what we say is important in the moment? There are lots of reasons, some more valid than others. Our own emergencies, other people's emergencies, lack of money, lack of time, insufficient information, no child care, our spouse, our boss, our kids—are all examples of excuses we use for not tending to our own needs. But regardless of the validity of our excuses, if we're really honest with ourselves, we see that most often it boils down to fear. We're afraid of what people will think of us if we put our needs above theirs. *Selfish* is the word that comes to mind.

On the airplane, the flight attendant reminds us, "If you are traveling with a child or someone who needs your assistance, put *your* oxygen mask on first, and *then* assist them." It's a good reminder that we do a better job of taking care of others if we first take care of ourselves.

Staying focused and on track is about keeping agreements with ourselves. Eventually, to succeed at what we want to do in life, we must start doing the things that lead to our success, regardless of life's distractions. We must be willing to take an action despite how we feel. We must stay focused on the goal.

This week, I invite you to have the courage to stay focused on your needs and desires—no matter what!

DAY 2

Identify three things you've put off doing. Perhaps it's mowing the lawn, cleaning out your closet or car trunk, finishing that proposal, meeting with your coach, getting started on your new health plan, going on that date, attending that networking event, or sending out that résumé. Whatever it is, this is the day to call it what it is: important unfinished business.

DAY 3

Create an intention to stay focused on what's important. Today write out a positive statement saying what you intend to do regarding those three things you've been putting off. For example, "I intend to go on that date" or "I will write that resume" or "I'm going to start my exercise plan."

DAY 4

Identify the task and break it into small pieces. What small steps can you take to get you started? If your room needs cleaning, you might start with picking up all the shoes on the floor and putting them in a closet. The next little step might be to pick up all the clothes from the floor. Making up your bed might be another task, and putting your books on the shelf might be another. Or, if your commitment is to write a book, you could begin by outlining the subtopics, creating a working title, and starting to write a few pages.

DAY 5

Schedule everything. In your date book or in your electronic calendar, schedule blocks of time—every week—to work on the small pieces that you've identified. It's more likely you'll follow through if you schedule the task.

DAY 6

If you've been diligent this week, you might already have accomplished a small goal. If so, why not repeat this cycle with the second of the tasks you've put off doing? If not, it's likely because of one of three things: you're trying to be perfect, you're waiting to get into the mood to take action, or you're afraid and don't know where to begin. Regardless of your excuse, just get started doing something. Sometimes the willingness to get started gets you motivated enough to take the next action. *Just do something!*

DAY 7

Finally it's day 7 again, your day to rest, recharge, regroup, and review your week. What observations can you make about your behavior this week? What worked? What didn't work? What day seemed extra hard? Why?

WEEK 9

Say No to Gossip

Thought for the Week

It's an esteemable act to say no to gossip.

Affirmations for the Week

I will take a proactive stand against gossip.

This week, I will not gossip about others.

Esteemable Actions for the Week

DAY 1

Recently I overheard someone who was sitting at the table next to mine talking on her cell phone.

"Who does she think she is?" the woman said. "Everyone at work knows she's sleeping with the boss. That's why she always gets special treatment."

There was a pause, as if the person on the other end of the phone was responding. Then the woman at the next table, somewhat frustrated, said, "I'm not gossiping, I'm just sharing some information. It's my opinion and I'm entitled to that."

As I watched and listened to this brief interaction, I wondered how often each of us engages in gossip. How many of you have ever heard such a statement? How many of you have ever made such a statement? More than just about anything, gossip compels the participants to take sides, creating a line between them and us. It's so destructive, yet we do it.

The key to recognizing gossip is motive. Why are you sharing information? Is it to compliment the person you're talking about? Are you sharing useful information or are you jealous and trying to get support in making fun of him or her? Have you ever been gossiped about? How did it feel? What was the basis of the comments? Were you ever able to overcome it? Did people treat you differently? Did it affect your job, family, or health?

If gossip is so hurtful and potentially harmful, why do we do it? First and foremost, because we can. For some people, it's as natural and easy as saying their name.

A second reason to gossip is because we often feel powerless over our lives, our jobs, our relationships. We feel ill equipped to confront the object of our anger, perhaps because he or she controls the purse strings or other needed resources. So we say things behind his or her back. Powerlessness breeds feelings of inadequacy and fear. When we're afraid or feel inadequate, we lash out in the only way we can—by making others feel as badly as we do. This takes the focus off our part in what happened and puts the blame squarely on someone else.

A third reason to gossip is because our lives may be boring and uninteresting. We look to the lives of other people to keep us entertained.

A fourth reason to gossip is because it creates alliances, a sense of camaraderie among the hurt and angry. Lines are drawn; sides are taken. It's them against us. And for us to really win and feel good about our win, we need others to align with our cause. When we join forces with the gossiper against someone else, we feel formidable and mighty. There is power in numbers. For the insecure person, being a part of the crowd works, whatever the cost.

Finally, gossipers don't feel good about themselves, and they want others to feel as badly as they do. We spend our days talking about another person, rather than living our lives or working at changing our condition. We become a part of the victim class, stuck in a downward spiral where the victim never really wins.

Regardless of the reason, gossip is the coward's way of dealing with feelings. It never resolves the issue. Instead, it takes away our power, fuels the flame, and garners support for our fear, ultimately making us feel angrier. Further, gossip hurts the gossiper as much as it does the person being talked about. While it may feel good in the moment to disparage someone else, deep down it damages our self-esteem. The energy we expend destroying someone's character could be used to change our own lives. And what goes around comes around. We get back what we put out.

So how do you break the pattern of gossip?

- Practice not uttering the first word of gossip. Once you start, it's hard to stop. Often people say to me, "But you don't understand, people won't like me or they'll start gossiping about me if I don't participate." As with any courageous act, stopping gossip, too, requires that you risk losing something, such as unhealthy friends. Again, courage is not an absence of fear; it's a willingness to walk through the fear. Don't utter the first word.

- Focus on living the life you want. If you're happy doing what you love or if you are at least making an effort to create the life you want, you won't have time to focus on the lives of others.

- Speak up for yourself in the moment. Having the courage to speak up—in the moment—when you feel slighted or hurt goes a long way to sidestepping gossip. The longer you hold on to your wounded feelings, the more ammunition you garner and the bigger your case for gossip.

- Walk away when people gossip around you. Gossipers need and thrive on willing participants. If no one is there, they won't talk.

And even if someone is there, that someone doesn't have to be you.

This week, you're invited to examine your behavior around gossip.

DAY 2

How has your behavior been regarding gossip during the last few days? Perhaps you found it necessary to talk about a neighbor, a co-worker, or a friend. Today identify three situations where you could have sidestepped the gossip, but didn't.

DAY 3

Today is a No-Gossip Esteemable Day. Practice not uttering the first word. It'll feel challenging in the beginning, but trust me. If you continue to practice not participating in gossip, it'll get easier and you'll feel better about yourself.

DAY 4

Today I want you to focus on living the life you want. What one action can you take today that moves you closer to taking back your power? When we gossip, we feel powerful, yet in truth, we become powerless. We give up our power every time we talk negatively about people who are living the life they love. What can you do that moves you closer to living the life you desire?

DAY 5

Today speak up for yourself or be more courageous in your actions. Do you feel you deserve a raise or a better job assignment? Why not ask for it, rather than gossiping about the boss or the co-worker who had the courage to speak up for what he or she wanted?

The other day I was standing in a long line waiting for one of two ATMs. The second was apparently broken because no one was using it. A woman walked ahead of the line to the machine that no one was using. Several people started growling and gossiping about the fact that she went past them to the machine. The truth is, the other line was empty and everyone assumed the second ATM was out of order. Not one person made an effort to determine whether the machine worked. This woman took an action to determine whether the ATM was operable. It was. She got her money and left. Was it the woman's fault that no one else took a moment to check the other machine? Was it her fault that everyone, including me, assumed the ATM didn't work?

DAY 6

From this day forward, focus on what you can do to avoid gossip. Every time you start to gossip, ask yourself, "Why am I doing it? What is the payoff? What's missing from my life that makes me want to talk about others?" Then ask yourself, "What can I do to change the situation?"

DAY 7

Day 7 is the Four Rs Day, a day for you to rest, recharge, regroup, and review your week. What observations can you make about your behavior his week? What worked? What didn't work? What day seemed extra hard?

WEEK 10

Courage to Make the Right Choice

Thought for the Week

You pay a price when you make poor choices.

Affirmations for the Week

I commit to making healthy choices.

This week, I am willing to make
the right choices.

Esteemable Actions for the Week

DAY 1

"I know the right thing to do," cried Marion. "I just don't want to do it."

"Yeah, I know smoking is bad for me," said Bill, "but it's my body and I'll do what I want with it."

"And no, the five cups of coffee I drank after dinner have nothing to do with my not being able to sleep. Mind your business," said Dan.

"I know I shouldn't have unprotected sex," said Whitney, "but my boyfriend just won't wear a condom."

"I know I shouldn't keep going back to him, but I love him," said Lena.

"I have a good idea, but I don't think anyone wants to hear it, so I keep it to myself," said Jimmy.

"I've put on so much weight that I'm embarrassed to go to the gym," said Joyce. "When I take off a few pounds, I'll start working out again."

Do any of these sound familiar?

Every day we make choices about how we want to live, feel, and behave. We make choices that affect our health, our finances, our relationships, and our well-being. And every day we feel the effects of those choices. And so do the people around us. Our choices don't exist in a vacuum.

There's a price we pay for poor choices. Added stress, strained relationships, dysfunctional homes, incorrigible kids, unhealthy bodies, and fewer desirable opportunities are among the consequences we pay. For example, Bill, by his choice, has increased his chances of lung cancer or any number of related health disorders. Joyce has gained fifty pounds, and her small frame is rebelling. Her back and legs ache, and at times she finds it hard to breathe. Yet she continues to choose cake, cookies, and ice cream and refuses to go to the gym. And Whitney, pregnant at fifteen, runs the risk of it happening again at seventeen.

When we make choices, we set in motion a cosmic reaction—one thing leads to another. Sometimes the outcome is what we want, but we're still unhappy. Sometimes we don't get what we want, yet the outcome turns out to be the best thing for us. How do we know when we're making the right choice? There's a quiet, small voice inside us that never lies or steers us in the wrong direction. The truth is that we always know right from wrong; sometimes we choose to ignore that knowledge. On occasion, we reject the right answer because it comes from a parent, teacher, spouse, or other perceived authority figure. There are also times when we pretend not to know what's appropriate, because we've decided to do what we want to do, no matter what.

So how do we go about making right choices? First, we get to the place of being willing to make right choices. We take a look at some recent decisions we've made and ask ourselves, "Is what I'm doing working for me? What consequences am I paying in order for me to feel good in the moment?" When our answers are honest and we are willing to see the truth, then we are ready to go to the next step: making better choices. At this juncture, we stop and listen to that intuitive voice. Often it competes with other, louder voices, voices that justify choices that are wrong for you. But despite the battle, deep down, we always know the right answer.

One of life's greatest gifts is realizing we have the power of choice. The idea that we can control what happens to us is liberating, yet at the same time powerfully frightening. Why? Because with choice comes responsibility. Self-esteem is about making choices for ourselves and being accountable for them. When we shirk that responsibility, we set ourselves up to be victims.

How easy it is to see ourselves as victims. How easy it is to do whatever we want in life, and then blame someone else for the outcome. This week is about making different choices, so we can bypass the victim role.

There are many things that get in the way of making right choices, such as addiction, out-of-control habits, sex, fear, feelings, other people's judgments, other people's power, family commitments, lack of money, and restricted time. And many bad decisions have been made in the name of love. Think back on Whitney: she's a mom at fifteen and well on her way to repeating the cycle. When does the insanity stop? When she becomes willing to make some different choices, such as using condoms regardless of whether her boyfriend likes them, finding a different boyfriend who genuinely cares about her well-being, or abstaining from sex.

So what choices are you making? This week, you're invited to examine your thought process for making decisions.

DAY 2

Bring to mind a decision you made in the last twenty-four hours. Perhaps it was to take a vacation or not, maybe it was to stick to your health plan or not, maybe it was to have a drink or not, maybe it was to vote or not, or maybe it was to leave home. What factors did you take into consideration? Write about that decision today.

DAY 3

Today is your Recognize Fear Day. A powerful foe, fear comes disguised in myriad ways. But regardless of its appearance, it affects your choices. Fear of risk, fear of pain, fear of failure, fear of success, fear of making a mistake, fear of being held accountable, fear of feeling inadequate, and fear of believing you really can't do what you say you can do are among the many fears that surface. When you're afraid, you make safe choices that are not always the best choices. Here's a story I once heard:

A spy was captured across enemy lines in a foreign land. The spy faced the captain, who was about to sentence him.

"In our country, spying is punishable by death," said the captain.

"I know," said the spy.

The captain said, "I'll give you two choices: you can die at the hands of the firing squad at dawn tomorrow or you can walk through that door." The captain pointed to a huge, ugly steel door with old rusty nails and bolts and grotesque carvings embedded into it.

Taking one look at the door, the spy gasped! "Can you give me until morning to decide? This is a hard choice to make." The captain agreed and sent the spy back to his cell until dawn.

At daybreak, the spy was returned and the captain asked, "Have you made your decision?"

The spy facing the captain said, "Yes, I have. Shoot me, because at least I know what I'm dealing with." The firing squad shot the spy.

Moments later, a medical volunteer who had observed the incident asked the captain, "What was behind the door? What could have been worse than death?"

The captain responded, "Behind the door was freedom, and the risk of the unknown."

Write about three specific instances when fear affected your decisions this week.

DAY 4

Today identify one example of how an addiction or bad habit has limited your choices or influenced your decisions. The addiction or bad habit could be yours or it could be someone else's that has affected you.

DAY 5

Today explore ways sex and relationships have affected your decisions. A client came to me recently, disturbed that her boyfriend left her. "I gave up everything for him," she cried. "I got rid of my cats because he didn't like them. I sent my kids to live with my parents. I stopped seeing my best friend because he thought she was too uppity. What should I do?" she cried. No doubt, from me, she needed love, support in that moment, and an understanding heart. She also needed to know she could have made some different choices early in the relationship. What choices have you made in the name of love or in pursuit of sex? Why did you make those choices? What was the outcome?

DAY 6

Often wrong choices are made because we don't ask questions. And if we do ask, we sometimes avoid the answers, which could enable us to make right choices. Think of an upcoming decision you need to make. List four or five questions you can ask that will assist you in making a better, more informed decision.

DAY 7

This was a tough week, and you did a great job! Now, on this seventh day, you rest, recharge, regroup, and review your week. What observations can you make about your ability to make different choices? What worked? What didn't work? What day seemed extra hard? Why? Now you're ready for the next week.

WEEK 11

Courage to Risk Failure

Thought for the Week

Self-esteem comes from having the courage
to risk failure.

Affirmations for the Week

If I fail, I get up, dust myself off,
and start all over again.

I am not a failure as long as I try.

Esteemable Actions for the Week

DAY 1

I've failed at many things in my life: driver's tests, school exams, relationships. Yes, indeed, I missed the mark more often than I care to
admit. I started fad diets and self-help programs and rarely got the
result I was after. I've bombed in front of audiences because I forgot
where I was going, was unprepared, or simply handled a situation
poorly. I know what it means to fail.

But nothing—absolutely nothing—has come close to how I felt
when I failed the New York Bar exam, the licensing exam for
lawyers. To date, it is the single most important failure I have ever
experienced. It was the first time I showed up, put myself on the
line, and missed the mark. It was the first time I did the work—even

in a small way. It was the first time I allowed myself to dream and dream big. Because the stakes were high, the fall was devastating. And because the fall was so demoralizing, the eventual victory was one to be savored.

Have you ever worked really hard toward reaching a goal, only to fail? Perhaps you failed a test, missed placement in an important competition, or had an important relationship end without your consent. Have you ever done your very best and your best just wasn't good enough? Perhaps you raised kids who grew up to hate you or, at best, turned into monsters. Have you ever sacrificed everything for someone else's dream and things didn't turn out the way you wanted them to? Maybe you put your spouse through school, and then he or she left after getting a degree. Have you ever given up on your dream so others could live theirs? Have you ever started on a journey and got a different result than you planned? If you answered yes to any of the above, this week is for you.

This week is about having the courage to risk failure, to be perceived as less than perfect, and to learn from your mistakes. It's about facing life on life's terms.

Society, media, and our schools tell us that if we fail, no one will like us, hire us, or want to be with us. It's no wonder many of us make safe choices to avoid the risk of failure. We simply give up and choose not to do anything that will subject us to an outcome where we won't be liked.

It's easy to give up, and it happens over time. One day we simply decide it's too hard to go for that dream of getting a college degree or starting our own business. Perhaps we decide we don't really want a promotion after all, that it's okay to make less money than we deserve. Or maybe we decide that that spouse who has been unfaithful for the hundredth time really needs our love and understanding. Settling for seconds in life becomes so easy that we slip into the "this is just fine" syndrome, and in some cases, we never know we're doing it. We go for the person with money instead of the person we love. Our manuscript sits on our desk, untouched for years, because we're afraid someone won't like it. Before we know it, our lives are all about safe choices.

With safe choices, we're not challenged to do anything we don't want to do. And some people believe we should never do what we don't want to do. There are few surprises, unplanned events, or obstacles to overcome. Indeed, with safe choices, there are no major bumps along the way and no major victories either.

On the other hand, there is something to be said for following our dreams, even when they take us into uncharted terrain. Knowing that we can accomplish a goal or acquire something we want adds a sweetness to life that no one can take away. Our blood, sweat, and tears went into the making of the miracle, and we earned it! No one likes to fail, whether it's making a mistake in public, getting divorced, being fired from a job, or as in my case, failing exams over and over again. But contrary to popular belief, failing is not the worst thing that could happen to us—not trying is.

It takes great courage to fail, because it takes great courage to try. It's hard to keep on keeping on when we're faced with one obstacle after another. Hard to stay the course when we feel weary and want to give up. It's difficult to turn the other cheek when we seem to continually get slapped in the face by defeat. Yet how often have we heard that the gift is in the journey? And indeed it is. But perhaps the real gift is to see failure not as a bad thing but as an opportunity to learn and grow into our best self.

Instead of making the safe choice, as a way to avoid failure, consider preparation as an alternative. Had I been better equipped for the Bar exam, perhaps I would have passed the first time. Unquestionably, there are times when no amount of prep work will save us, but it's amazing how often a little groundwork can help us circumvent repeated visits of failure.

So this week, your focus will be on taking risks, some small and some great. The small baby steps are as significant as the bigger steps. Each action step counts.

DAY 2

This is the day for admitting mistakes. Bring to mind a failed experience, a mistake, or a time you were rejected. What happened? How could you have handled it differently?

DAY 3

Most often we don't go for our dreams because we're afraid to fail, make a mistake, or be rejected. Today you're invited to revisit your top three dreams. What obstacles prevent you from realizing those dreams? Your initial response might be lack of money, lack of education, no time, no child care. But I encourage you to go deeper to the fear underneath. What's the real reason? Write out your answers in your esteemable acts journal.

DAY 4

Take action today. Do something you've put off doing. Send out your résumé, write your book proposal, register for a class, complete your manuscript, learn a new skill, ask for that well-deserved raise, request a more challenging work assignment, go for your number-one dream, or ask for help in doing these things.

DAY 5

Today do two things you've put off because you're afraid of the outcome. They could be little things, although what might be little to one person is monumental to another. One of my clients is afraid to take the escalator. She has avoided escalators all her life and paid a price for her fear. Fear has limited her choices in activities with friends and family. Last week, she took the escalator in the subway.

She risked making a mistake or looking foolish. That's an esteemable act!

DAY 6

This week, do one more thing you're afraid to do. Select a task that's really been a thorn in your side, something that embarrasses or frustrates you. I know I'm asking a lot this week, and I know you can do it. Just imagine how fabulous you'll feel after you've done it.

DAY 7

This is your Four Rs Day, the day when you rest, recharge, regroup, and review your week. What observations can you make about your behavior this week? What did you learn from your experiences? What day seemed extra hard? Why?

WEEK 12

Learn a New Skill

Thought for the Week

It's an esteemable act to have the courage to learn
something new.

Affirmations for the Week

I am willing to learn a new skill.

This week, I will do something I'm not yet good at.

Esteemable Actions for the Week

DAY 1

Have you ever avoided doing something because it was too hard or
too scary? Have you ever not learned a new skill because you were
afraid you'd make a mistake or just look silly? If you're like most of
us, you've been there—done that. And like many people, you've
missed out on a great deal of fun and opportunity because you were
afraid to learn something new.

Think of things you're good at, such as dancing, skiing, swim-
ming, using a computer, driving a car, staying sober, managing your
team, or writing songs. Now remember the first time you did that
activity. I bet you weren't very good. Actually, if you're like me, you
had to try, try, and try again before you got into the swing of things.
Am I right? Yet it was the conscious, consistent practice of that new

skill that ultimately made you proficient and confident that you could do it. Think about how good you felt when you finally got it right.

No question about it, learning a new skill is hard, it's scary, and at times it's embarrassing. But recall your reward every time you did something you didn't think you could do. It's a thrill to learn. It's something no one can take away from you. You earned the right to say, "I know what I'm doing."

In 1996, I learned how to use e-mail. I had started the process in 1994. Obviously I wasn't a fast learner. Over and over I tried, and over and over I got it wrong. I felt so stupid because everyone around me seemed to get it on the first try. They made it seem easy, but for me, it was a nightmare. Forget about using e-mail, I couldn't even install the software.

I didn't fare much better when learning to use my VCR. Nor was it a day at the park when I tried to learn how to make changes to my Web site. Technology is my challenge area, the area where, if given a chance, I would give up before getting started. But it wasn't the only area where I risked looking stupid and made lots of mistakes. I speak for a living, and people say things like, "You're so inspirational," "You're such a good speaker," "You never seem afraid," "How can you get up there and tell those things about yourself?" Yet for every time I do well on the platform, there are memories of times I bombed, and bombed big time.

One painful memory was when I was invited to speak at an event for thirty minutes. I froze as I looked into the audience of nine hundred people. I couldn't believe I was expected to talk to that many people for that period of time. I cried, went blank, and, five minutes later, sat down embarrassed and ashamed. It was the first of many more similar embarrassing moments, some equally as memorable.

In the past, each time I tried something new and didn't get it the first time, I wanted to give up. It felt like the end of my world. But I didn't give up. There are even days when I know what I'm doing and still feel like I'm off the beam. And on those days, I just don't give up. Today I know whatever I'm experiencing is part of my learning process, whether it's using my computer or speaking in front of an audience. My job is to remain teachable.

The following are tips on learning a new skill:

- Be teachable. The hardest thing for some of us is to admit we don't know. Yet the first step in any improvement process is being teachable: admitting you don't know something and asking for help.
- Ask for help. Have the courage to seek out help from those who know, whether from a life coach, consultant, specialist, classroom instructor, or anyone else with the skills you need.
- Allow yourself to make mistakes. You don't have to do it perfectly the first time, or the first five times. There is always a learning curve to developing a new skill. Often it's in making mistakes that you get to understand the process.
- Practice your new skill. There's much truth to the saying "practice makes perfect." But I like to say "practice makes better." The more you practice your new skill, the better you become.

This week, you're invited to learn a new skill.

DAY 2

Today is your Identify New Skills Day. Identify three skills that would make you a better employee, parent, spouse, or simply a more rounded person. Perhaps this week, you'll sign up for that college or computer class. What about classes on riding horses, playing piano, painting, or cooking? Whatever it is, think of something you'd like to learn. This week, you have permission to go for it.

DAY 3

Today identify places you'll go to learn your new skill. Local high schools, colleges, or technical training institutes are valuable resources. Community recreation centers, libraries, and local YMCAs or YWCAs also offer skill-building classes. In some communities, you'll find the Learning Annex, the Knowledge Bank, or other organizations that offer low-cost classes in skills training.

DAY 4

Today is your Sign Up for a Class Day. Sign up for that class or make an appointment with the person who has knowledge or information to share. Some classes will begin immediately; others may not start for a few weeks. Regardless, pay the fee and sign up before you change your mind.

DAY 5

In your date book, schedule several days a week—every week—to work on your new skill. It's more likely you'll follow through if you schedule it.

DAY 6

This is Begin Your Schedule Day. Spend an hour today practicing your new skill. The more you do it, the easier it will become. You can do it.

DAY 7

Today is the Four Rs Day: rest, recharge, regroup, and review your week. What observations can you make about your behavior this week? What worked? What didn't work? Which day seemed extra hard? Why? You'll feel better about yourself if you *just do it*!

Personal Inventory

Thought for the Week

It's an esteemable act to see yourself clearly.

Affirmations for the Week

I welcome the opportunity to know myself better.

This week, I am willing to see the part I play
in my interactions with others.

Esteemable Actions for the Week

DAY 1

It's easy to be grateful when you receive compliments because they validate who we are and who we want to be. Positive feedback feels good. And some people believe we should only be given encouraging, appreciative feedback. However, while positive feedback is satisfying, it doesn't always help us get to where we want to be. To succeed, we must be willing to hear what works *and* what could make us even more effective. For example, for a business to thrive and be financially stable, it must be open to continual examination of its assets and liabilities. Often, in order for a business to see itself clearly, it needs to hire outside consultants. It is the same with us. The key is to select someone we trust to tell us the truth.

I, too, need to be prepared to hear the truth in my business. I'm usually very organized, especially for my presentations. I prepare carefully, and on the day of the event, I arrive early enough to set up without stress. But not long ago I blew it. And there was no excuse valid enough to justify it. While I was prepared for the event, I arrived to the meeting room only thirty minutes before the session. There was little time to double-check my equipment, and as luck would have it, I encountered a problem. Due to this last-minute mishap, I appeared disorganized and scattered. My evaluations reflected that sentiment.

There was a time when I would have been devastated to receive negative feedback on an evaluation. I would have been obsessed with the thought that I was perceived as less than perfect. I also would have anxiously tried to explain to my critic that normally I was extremely prepared, even if not today. But I've changed. Now I ask myself, "Is there truth in that criticism?" And in this particular case, there was.

I want to be the best I can be, which requires me to be open to the truth about what works and what doesn't work in my life. Having the courage to identify areas in need of improvement is an esteemable act.

When we see ourselves clearly, we gain a greater sense of freedom because our character defects can, and do, control us. The more we deny their existence, the more control they have. Self-knowledge can also free us from secrets. We are as sick as our secrets, as the saying goes. The more secrets we keep, the more imprisoned we feel. The more imprisoned we feel, the more our character defects surface. Finally, self-knowledge enhances our ability to love others. The more willing we are to receive feedback, the more human we become. The more human we become, the more we can connect with the humanity of others.

There are many reasons for not wanting to know the truth. Perhaps we're afraid of what we might find, or we're afraid people will judge us. Maybe we have an investment in maintaining a certain image, or we're afraid people won't like us once they know who we are.

So how do we get past the obstacles? We take an action by following these steps:

1. Do an inventory of your personal strengths and weaknesses.
2. Ask for feedback from friends and co-workers.
3. Identify conflicts with others and ask, "What part did I play?"
4. When someone gives you feedback or criticism, ask yourself, "Could what they say be true?"

DAY 2

Today is your Inventory Day. It's a day when you take stock of what works and what doesn't. Let's begin with your strengths. Identify six of your strengths; these are traits that make you likable, productive, and effective as a parent, spouse, employee, or friend. Sometimes we're afraid to admit things we do well, for fear someone will think we're conceited. No one will read this but you, so don't worry. Just do it!

DAY 3

Today let's continue your inventory. Identify six of your challenges: these are traits that, if improved, would make you even more effective than you already are. Be as honest as you can. Everyone has areas that need improvement.

DAY 4

Today let's focus on ways you use guilt to your advantage. Guilt, that ghastly feeling we're taught to run from, can sometimes tell us when something is wrong and needs to be corrected. Sometimes it's easier to talk about feeling guilty than changing the behavior that makes us feel guilty. Early in my recovery, I complained to my sponsor how guilty I felt. Knowing my situation all too well, she simply said, "If you hate feeling guilty, stop doing the things that make you feel guilty, like sleeping with other women's husbands." What a novel concept! What do you feel guilty about? What positive and appropriate actions can you take to alleviate the guilt?

DAY 5

Today you're invited to really step outside your comfort zone and solicit feedback from others. No doubt this is one of the most courageous things you'll ever do. You will get valuable information about how to be the best you can be, and you will get to walk through your fear.

When was the last time you asked a friend what you could do to be a better friend? When was the last time you elicited feedback from your supervisor on how to improve your work? Or asked your co-workers or spouse what you could do to be a more effective team player? When was the last time you invited feedback from people in your audience? It's hard to open up to feedback, but when we do, we give ourselves a gift. Unless you hear how you affect others, you're likely to think you don't. And if you think your behavior doesn't affect others, you'll believe there is no need to change. It's an esteemable act to have the courage to hear the truth and do something about it.

DAY 6

By now you're getting a better sense of yourself, and for a moment, you might even start to think you're the worst person in the world. Well, you're not; you're just a work in progress. Don't let your feelings get in the way of the work to be done. Today is your opportunity to improve. Think of two things you can do to become more effective than you already are. Now go do them.

DAY 7

We're at day 7, your day to rest, recharge, regroup, and review your week. What observations can you make about your willingness to see yourself clearly? Was the idea of accepting feedback challenging? What worked? What didn't work? What day seemed extra hard? Why?

Pamper Yourself

Thought for the Week

It's an esteemable act to take time
to pamper yourself.

Affirmations for the Week

I deserve to pamper myself.

This week, I will do something nice for myself.

Esteemable Actions for the Week

DAY 1

For her birthday, I gave my friend Caryn a gift certificate for a half
day of spa treatments, including a massage, manicure, pedicure, and
facial. "What a great gift," I thought, "because it is something she'd
never give to herself." But when I handed it to her, she looked at me
as if I had given her poison.

"What am I supposed to do with this?" she asked.

"Call to schedule an appointment, show up, and enjoy yourself,"
I said.

"Thanks for the gift, but I'm going to pass. I don't have time to
take four hours out of my day to pamper myself," she retorted.

"Why not, Caryn?" I asked. "At least for this once?" I was really interested in hearing her excuses, so I repeated the question, "Why not?"

"Francine, I'm just too busy with the kids. You know my life. When would I have time to take four hours out of my day for me? The kids would think I was selfish if I wasn't there after school one day. And my husband, well, you know Kenny, he'd probably think I was having an affair if I got massaged, painted, and soaked for half a day. I mean why else would I spend that kind of time on me?"

I couldn't believe what I was hearing. Yet not too many years earlier, I had been just like Caryn. She was typical, as I had been. Sadly, my gift to a friend turned into a conversation about how selfish it is to pamper ourselves.

She reluctantly accepted my gift. Then, after her half day of spa treatments, she came to me and said, "I don't know why it took me so long to do this. Thank you for giving me this gift." I was amazed and grateful that my friend had learned the value of self-care, as I had years earlier. Now, every few months, she gives herself the gift of a half day of pampering.

When it comes to self-care, we first must confront some destructive cultural beliefs. Many of us grew up in families that viewed self-care as selfish, self-centered, or just for the wealthy. Our beliefs can be so powerful that, if challenged, we go on the attack, almost like a mother protecting her young.

As for women, many of us have been socialized to believe our sole job is to be there for others. We're taught our primary role in life is to be a wife, a mother, or somebody's caretaker. The very idea of taking care of ourselves is so far beyond anything we could imagine that it scares us, and in many cases, offends us. As women, we feel guilty if we take even an hour for ourselves. This doesn't just apply to stay-at-home moms. How often do working women work right through lunch?

While men are given a little more permission to tend to their needs, many men still grow up with the belief that they must be good little soldiers. So often, they work too hard and neglect their health because it's the "right thing" to do. Then, after years of pent-up feelings, they retaliate through drinking, adultery, or leaving the family emotionally. When we ignore our needs for so long, eventually we and those around us suffer.

This week, you're invited to temporarily suspend your beliefs about self-care. You're invited to emotionally splurge this week, take a bubble bath or two and get a manicure, pedicure, or facial. And yes, that applies to men as well. This week, you're invited to spend quiet time with you and maybe even sleep thirty minutes later. If you've never done this before, it'll be a little challenging but worth the effort. If you are accustomed to pampering yourself, then this week you have permission to do it again.

DAY 2

Today and every day this week, take thirty minutes for quiet time. Maybe it's after you send the kids off to school, after they've been put to bed, or during your lunch hour. Regardless, create that space for yourself this week. A daily spiritual practice of quiet time creates a balance between the *doing* and the *being* aspects of your life. It doesn't matter what your daily practice looks like, as long as you choose something. It could be meditation, prayer, or even yoga. Just spend some time alone with you this week—no kids, no spouse, no television, no work, just you.

DAY 3

Today spend an extra fifteen minutes in bed after your alarm goes off. You don't have to do anything, just lie there. Think about how good it feels to really experience your bed and not jump out of it when the alarm goes off.

DAY 4

Today I invite you to go on retreat. This could mean a day without running errands, checking e-mail, checking voice mail, or doing fix-it projects around the house. It could mean a day without the kids. It could be mean a day where you simply take a walk in the park by yourself. This is your day to take it easy and make space for you.

Let's fill today with small luxuries, such as taking a long bubble bath, curling up in bed with a good book, or watching your favorite reruns on television. You're probably thinking, "Who has the time to do that?" If you are ever going to have the time for yourself, you must make the time. It won't just happen. For those of us who put everyone's needs above our own, we have to work at it. It's a mindset that must be temporarily suspended—one day at a time.

DAY 5

If you can, schedule a massage today. If money is an issue, then call a local massage school to find out what student services are offered to the public at reduced prices.

DAY 6

Today why not do something really bold? Go to the cosmetic counter of your local department store and sign up for a free makeover, just for the fun of it. Or, if you can afford it, buy yourself a new nightgown. If you are a man, go to your favorite men's store and buy a new shirt or new tie.

DAY 7

Day 7 is the Four Rs Day, a day for you to rest, recharge, regroup, and review your week. What observations can you make about your openness to being pampered? Was the idea of self-care challenging? What worked? What didn't work? What day seemed extra hard? Why?

WEEK 15

Service: Freely Given, Freely Received

Thought for the Week

It's an esteemable act to give freely of yourself.

Affirmations for the Week

I am open to sharing my gifts with others.

This week, I give freely of what I've been given.

Esteemable Actions for the Week

DAY 1

Imagine you've lived a long, full life, and now you find yourself at the pearly gates. Upon arrival, the gatekeeper doesn't ask how many pairs of cute shoes you have, where you went to school, how much money is in your stock portfolio, or how many children you raised. Instead you're asked, "Who did you help? How were you of service to others? How did you use your life to benefit others?" The very idea of one person helping another dates as far back as the beginning of civilization.

This week, you're invited to explore the concept of service and what it means to have a consciousness of giving. Everyone has something to give, regardless of how small or seemingly unimportant the gift may appear. A simple offer of kindness can make someone's day. Service takes many forms, such as offering a smile when someone feels unlovable, appreciating someone's effort, or spending time with a friend who needs to be heard without judgment. It may be sharing your skill or expertise with someone new to your career field, welcoming a new neighbor into the community, holding the door for the person behind you, or saying thank you to the one who held the door for you. There are many ways to serve.

As far back as I can remember, I've been the poster child for someone who is selfish, self-centered, and self-absorbed. I've spent my life asking, "What is in it for me?" I tried to figure out how others could help me, rather than what I could do for them. Getting sober changed my attitude, not because I wanted to be a giving person but because I realized I had to help other suffering alcoholics if I was to stay sober. The more I gave, the more I got back in return. What a concept.

Developing a consciousness of giving is hard at first, especially if we're used to being a taker. But while the process of change is not easy, the formula is simple: willingness + time = a shift in our thinking. Every experience becomes an opportunity for service. Sometimes we give for the sake of giving and sometimes we give because we know that when we succeed as a collective group, we succeed as individuals.

There are many benefits to being of service to others. It's rewarding to watch a person's face light up when you help him or her achieve something he or she thinks is impossible. My personal niche area is working with women and mentoring teenage girls. It's a pleasure when I see them experience that "aha" moment, particularly when I know that in some small way I helped. Another benefit is that service to others allows us to make amends for past mistakes, particularly if it's impossible to make a direct amend to the person we harmed. Service to others helps us make new friends. We automatically become connected to a community of like-minded people. One great question to start a conversation is "What organizations do you support?" Giving freely of what we've been given also softens our heart and warms our spirit. We become nicer people because we care about others. Finally, service is a way to get through the tough times. Each time I faced a major challenge, it was my service work that enabled me to get through it because I shared my pain and used my experience, strength, and hope to help someone else.

With all the benefits, there are still reasons why many people don't get involved in service activities. Not having enough time is the reason I hear most often. Yet the good news about service is we get to choose what we do and to what extent. "It costs too much and I don't have the time," said Jacquie, a woman I coach. Money is not the only way to give, and as for time, we choose when, where, what, and how we give.

Are you like Jacquie, trapped in the belief that giving requires big actions, such as paying someone's rent, buying dinner, sharing your personal belongings, giving thousands of dollars to charity, or volunteering many hours of your precious time? It can include those actions, but it's the act of giving that is big. Giving doesn't take much, just a willingness to give is enough. Doing someone's laundry, running an errand, or preparing a meal for someone who's ill is an act of giving. Taking out the garbage without being asked, volunteering to help out a neighbor who works long hours, or offering to pick up the kids are all examples of things we can do in the name of helping another person. Spending time with a friend, listening without judgment, or putting money in someone's expired parking meter are other ways to serve.

Maybe today your gift is simply refraining from making an obscene gesture or cutting someone off in traffic. Maybe it's having the courage to forgive an unforgivable person or treating someone with kindness even when there's no crisis. Maybe it's not participating in gossip, or being a voice against gossip. Perhaps your act of service is being an example of courage. Courage breeds courage.

Each time you have the courage to do the right thing, you give someone else permission to do the same. That's an act of service.

This week, you're invited to step, with both feet, into a world where service to others reigns supreme.

DAY 2

Today is your day for being open to opportunities for service. The opening of your heart creates a space for giving. When the space is created, opportunities abound. Pray for the willingness to see what they are. You could be walking down the street and see an opportunity to give. You could be at work and see an opportunity to serve. You could be in traffic or in the line at the supermarket and come face to face with an opportunity to be of service. There are people and situations everywhere that cry out for your gift of caring. This is your day for being on the lookout for ways to help others.

DAY 3

Today is an Esteemable Service Day. Go find two people to help. Offer to carry a bag, help someone across the street, stop and listen without appearing hurried. You get to choose how you want to give. This morning I woke up to a torrential rain and had plans to meet a friend. I would have been justified in postponing our meeting, but I knew today I needed to show up. And I did. As it turned out, today was a day she really needed a friend. I'm glad I was there for her. There may be days when I'll really need to call and postpone an appointment, but today I knew it was right for me to show up.

DAY 4

Today stretch yourself just a little and offer help where you wouldn't normally or in ways you would normally not give. Don't overextend yourself to the point where it's a financial, emotional, or physical hardship. Do what is realistic for you, but be willing to step outside your comfort zone on occasion for someone else.

DAY 5

Today practice being a receiver-centered giver. Give with the other person in mind. Give what they need or want, not what you think they should have. My husband is a sensitive guy. And while he loves tools and gadgets as gifts, he also appreciates when I'm sweet, kind, and value his effort. At times, that's a better gift than anything I could buy.

DAY 6

This is Maintain Your Balance Day. The other side of doing nothing is doing too much. We overextend, often because we are afraid to say no or we love what we do so much we lose sight of the need for balanced self-care. Don't let doing too much for others translate into neglect of yourself. While no doubt it's easier to say than to do, with practice, you can take better care of yourself. How are you balancing your desire to help others with your need for self-care?

DAY 7

We're at day 7, your day to rest, recharge, regroup, and review your week. What observations can you make about your thinking this week? Was the idea of service challenging? What worked? What didn't work? What day seemed extra hard? Why?

WEEK 16

Your Finances Are Your Responsibility

Thought for the Week

Self-esteem comes from taking responsibility
for your finances.

Affirmations for the Week

I deserve to be debt free.

This week, I will act as if I am a financially
responsible person.

Esteemable Actions for the Week

DAY 1

My friend Jack's finances and his life are out of control. He's got
$36,000 worth of credit-card debt and a mortgage that exceeds his
monthly salary, his kids are in a private school he can't afford, he
drives a current-year luxury car, he drinks lattes seven days a week
and eats out almost as often. He sees his life as normal, and he can't
understand why it feels so unmanageable.

Financial freedom is a result of effectively managing our finances, and the way we handle our finances is the way we handle
our lives. Are you having difficulty managing your personal affairs?
Do you feel lost and confused more often than you'd like? Do you

feel like other people are in control of your life? Do you feel powerless? If your attention is glued to this page, I bet your money is also in a state of imbalance.

How do we get out of balance regarding our finances? By making poor choices over an extended period of time. It simply doesn't happen overnight. We spend a little beyond our means and needs one day, then we do it again the next day. Before we know it, we're in debt and can't understand why.

What compels us to make poor choices? First, it's our beliefs about money. Some of our beliefs about money include the following:

- "Money is the root of all evil."
- "Money solves all problems."
- "Once in debt, always in debt."
- "Hard work gets you nowhere."
- "Money can buy anything."
- "Looking good is everything."
- "We must keep up with the Joneses."

Second, fear compels us to make poor choices. We feel inadequate and afraid of what people will think of us. We want to keep up with the Joneses and look a certain way to impress others. We want to have the biggest and best house on the block, send our kids to the most prestigious school, drive the most awesome vehicle, and lay claim to the most incredible array of techno gadgets. Indeed, fear plays a major part in financial instability. And while in the moment it feels good to have these things, ultimately it's hard to sustain that feeling when we're saddled with debt, we can't pay our bills, and our income doesn't adequately cover our expenses.

What about you? When the topic of money comes up, are you uncomfortable? Do you think, "I wish they'd change the subject?" Do you get defensive? If so, this week is tailor-made for you.

How do we get past the belief system that obliges us to live irresponsibly? We take action, and lots of it. Here are a few suggestions:

- Pay yourself first. Stash 10 percent of your paycheck away: just save it. Don't spend it. Don't make it a rainy day fund. Just save it. Some of you might think, "I can't afford to save 10 percent." Then save 5 percent or whatever you can. Just start somewhere. Think of how much change you have at the bottom of your purse or in your pockets. Think of how much money you leave lying around on the floor or in drawers. Think of how many lattes, Cokes, or packs of cigarettes you purchase. Not buying one four-dollar latte, seven days a week, for fifty-two weeks a year adds up. Do the math. You could put that little savings in a "No Latte Today" fund. It all adds up. Something is better than nothing, and it gets you in the habit of saving. Save what you can, but save something.
- Spend less. Just because it's there doesn't mean you should buy it. There are times when you need to practice restraint and not spend.
- Avoid debt. Not a difficult concept to grasp, but one that eludes many people. In our buy-now-pay-later society, we're encouraged to amass debt at whatever cost. For example, credit-card companies tantalize graduate students with the promise of a quick fix before they are even capable of supporting themselves. And this strategic campaign is not just reserved for graduate students. Credit-card companies send appealing invitations to students who are still in school. They learn to say "Charge it!" before they have a job. Spending beyond your income or when you have no income is a surefire way to financial insecurity, not financial freedom. Debt is not your friend and neither is the creditor.

This week, you're invited to examine your behavior around money: how you spend it, why you spend so much of it, where you spend it, and what you need to do to manage your money and your life a little better.

DAY 2

Today you get to identify your financial goals. What are your three top financial goals? They might be to get out of debt, own your own home, pay for college for your kids, have a retirement nest egg, or buy investment property. Where would you like to be financially in five, ten, and twenty years? Write about it.

DAY 3

This is your Assess Your Financial Situation Day. Today requires a lot of honesty. How much income do you have? What is your weekly take-home salary? Do you have a pension? Do you receive social security, stock dividends, alimony, allowances, interest, rental income, royalties, or tax refunds? Do you have other sources of income? Next, how do you spend your money? Housing, telephone, utilities, car payments, car maintenance, gas, other transportation costs, eating out, entertainment, health and wellness, education, savings and investments, business-related expenses, charitable donations, lattes? What percentage of your money goes to each category?

What assets do you own, such as a home, car, boat, computer, business equipment, copyrights, and trademarks? What are your liabilities? What do you owe? Do you have balances on your credit cards? Do you have student loans? The quickest and most effective way to find out what you owe is to get a credit report. Credit reporting companies will send you a copy of your report for a fee. Record your answers.

DAY 4

This is your Learn Something New Day. Sometimes we find ourselves in trouble because we don't have adequate information. Today I invite you to walk through your fear and get some financial information. There are many resources available. Utilize the Internet, the public library, and friends and associates with personal experience.

The reference librarian at your local library can be your best friend. Start reading articles and books that make finances easy to understand, and don't be afraid to look up a word you don't understand. Be bold, read the financial pages in the *Wall Street Journal* or the finance column in your favorite magazine. Commit to doing one thing today toward enhancing your financial knowledge.

DAY 5

Get help. Don't be afraid to ask for assistance in identifying solutions. Like your health, remember, your finances are your responsibility, so select your financial guides as carefully as you would a physician. And regardless of what they tell you, it's your responsibility to ask questions and weigh the pros and cons.

DAY 6

What one thing can you do today to improve your financial situation? Perhaps you were surprised to discover that you spend $500 a year on lattes, 10 percent of your income on clothes you never wear, or $100 over your budget for eating out. What different choices can you make today?

DAY 7

This was a tough week, and you did a great job! Now, on this seventh day, you rest, recharge, regroup, and review your week. What observations can you make about your behavior this week? What worked? What didn't work? What day seemed extra hard? Why? What did you get from this esteemable acts experience? Now you're ready for the next week.

Your Health Is Your Business

Thought for the Week

Good health is not a right, it's a privilege.

Affirmations for the Week

I can take responsibility for my health.

This week, I will act as if I like my body.

Esteemable Actions for the Week

DAY 1

As a teenager, I was convinced that my body was indestructible, like those of the television characters I idolized: Batgirl and Wonder Woman. I lived on a diet of hamburgers, french fries, macaroni and cheese, soda, alcohol, and cigarettes. And my habits didn't change much as I grew older. I just added more expensive foods, such as fine wine and rich pastas. The only time I went to the doctor was when I was forced to go. My health, in my mind, was someone else's responsibility. Obviously, it wasn't mine.

So it should come as no surprise that, after years of poor habits and addiction, I pay the price for my previous lifestyle and twisted belief system. Despite twenty-six years of recovery, I have physical scars that will never go away. Sometimes the price I pay is chronic back pain, sometimes it's that I can't move parts of my body with complete range of motion, sometimes it's that I must reread material several times to understand it, and sometimes it's just hard to breathe through my nose because I smoked three packs of cigarettes a day for sixteen years. I haven't had a cigarette since 1982. It has taken me years to understand, but today I know my health is my responsibility.

Good health is not a right, it's a privilege. And with privilege comes responsibility. For many of us, it's only when we lose our health that we realize how important it is. I have a friend who has lung cancer. He has smoked cigarettes for twenty-seven years. That could be me—or you.

What gets in the way of good health? Damaging beliefs that suggest our health is someone else's responsibility, fear, laziness, lack of information, an it-can't-happen-to-me attitude, and a wait-and-see attitude are all among the obstacles.

I recently asked a group of people how many believed their health was their responsibility. All hands flew up.

"Absolutely!" said one woman. "It's my job to take care of my health."

"Who else is supposed to take care of it?" someone else yelled out.

"What a silly question," said a third person. "Of course my health is my responsibility."

And yet as the session went on, most of the respondents left me wondering whether they really believed what they said. Two were overweight, several smoked at the break, and one person shared his fear of confronting his doctor about medication he was prescribed. It's easy to say we are responsible, but the evidence is in our actions— and our actions don't lie. Knowing something is your responsibility and really accepting responsibility are not one and the same. We accept responsibility when we do something about it. In some cases, that means ceasing damaging behavior.

Fear of what we might find is another reason we don't take care of ourselves. For years I refused to get an AIDS test, even after years of illicit sexual behavior. It was fear of what I'd find that stopped me. Not knowing seemed safer than knowing. Lack of time is another reason used for not taking responsibility for our health. One of my clients admitted she hadn't had a checkup in sixteen years.

"Why not?" I asked.

"Because I never had the time," she answered.

"Didn't have the time?" I asked. "How could you not have the time to go to the doctor?"

"I work," she said, "have kids, and a husband to take care of. Who has the time to go to the doctor?" The truth is, if she doesn't take care of herself, she won't have to worry about her job, kids, or husband. Our health is our responsibility.

Finally, one of my other clients went to the doctor for an annual checkup but refused to do regular self-testing for breast cancer. She forgot or just didn't feel like it or didn't have the time. Last year, she was diagnosed with breast cancer. Was lack of information her problem? Was the lack of a self-exam the cause? Doubtful, yet had she regularly examined herself and gotten mammograms, perhaps the cancer could have been detected sooner.

Yes, sometimes lack of time, lack of knowledge, or lack of funds can be an obstacle. But thanks to the Internet, the public library, magazines, books, and yes, even television, information is readily available and free. As for lack of money, local clinics provide a variety of services for free. All we have to do is ask for help.

Another obstacle to taking care of our health is the belief that nothing can happen to us. We may think that we can treat our bodies any way we want and not have to deal with the consequences.

The final obstacle to taking care of our health is a wait-and-see attitude. We wait to see if the problem goes away, despite evidence suggesting we should take care of it now. Sometimes we think that if we ignore it, the problem will go away. More often than not, it gets bigger.

This week, you're invited to explore ways to take better care of your health. For some of you, it will mean moving your body, drinking more water, or reducing the amount of food you eat. For others, it will mean eating more or getting a checkup. Let's get ready for a healthful experience this week.

DAY 2

Good health is a result of choices: smart, courageous, proactive, well-thought-out choices. These choices invite you to say yes when others say no, and invite you to say no when others say yes. What smart, courageous, proactive, or well-thought-out choices regarding your health did you make in the last twenty-four hours?

DAY 3

Today is your Assessment Day. The first step in changing poor health habits is to evaluate honestly the shape your health is in. What do you eat? Do you regularly exercise? Are you overweight? Do you have poor habits, such as drinking, smoking, or doing drugs? When was the last time you had a regular physical? What medical exams or screenings have you had? What's your family's health history? What do you need to know and how can you get the information you need? Answer these questions today. The second phase of this exercise is to secure a current photograph of yourself. The more clearly you see yourself, the sooner you can move toward better self-care.

DAY 4

Today is your day for gathering information that will help you live a healthier life. Perhaps there are tests you need, such as for AIDS and other sexually transmitted diseases, blood pressure, bone density, cholesterol, flu, glucose, hearing, and vision. Others might include a breast exam, fecal occult blood test, mammogram, Pap smear, prostate-specific antigen test, or thyroid-stimulating hormone measurement. Start with the Internet—it's a wonderful resource—then the public library, magazines, and reference books. The more you know, the more you can help yourself. This is an important step in taking care of your health. What tests do you need?

DAY 5

Today schedule an appointment with your doctor or a clinic. Additional actions you can take today are to eat smaller portions, drink more water, use the stairs rather than the elevator, eat more vegetables, track your food, and avoid sugar. This is your day for small actions.

DAY 6

Today read an article related to health. Select something of interest to you, and identify one thing you learned from the article. How will you apply your new knowledge?

DAY 7

Today is your day to rest, recharge, regroup, and review your week. What observations can you make about your behavior regarding your health? What worked? What didn't work? What day seemed extra hard? Why?

WEEK 18

Tell Your Story

Thought for the Week

Self-esteem comes from having the courage
to tell your story.

Affirmations for the Week

I deserve to be free from my past.

This week, I don't regret my past nor wish
to shut the door on it.

Esteemable Actions for the Week

DAY 1

Everyone has a story. Regardless of what our lives look like today,
we have a history. For many of us, recalling certain times in our lives
is painful. We'd rather forget our history. We'd rather put a lid on it.
But in truth, it doesn't go away. It simply lies in wait until it is given
permission to resurface again. And make no mistake about it, it will
resurface. Until we truly make peace with our history, it never goes
away. To heal, we must forgive ourselves but not forget the past.

Why do we want it to go away? Because we hope that out of
sight means out of mind. Somehow we think if we aren't living the
experience today, it no longer exists. We are also afraid people will
judge us or use our past against us. We may fear we'll lose friends,

family, and job opportunities. Another reason is we don't want to feel the feelings that surface as we recall our past lives. Shame, self-loathing, guilt, disappointment, and betrayal are among the feelings we'd prefer to avoid. And sadly for some, we believe if we remember our past transgressions, we minimize the accomplishments we've given birth to since that time.

But the truth is that before we can truly get past the hurt of what came before, we must acknowledge and accept it. That requires the delicate balance between time and action. It has been proven that time by itself doesn't erase pain. Think about your own experience. Bring to mind someone—years ago—you didn't like. Perhaps five, ten, or even twenty years have passed. When the thought of that person comes up or someone mentions his or her name, how does your gut feel? Unless you've done some serious work, it's likely the pain is as strong as it was years ago.

But often action too quickly engaged doesn't get us past the sting of our past either. Think of all the times you thought if you did everything right today, you'd feel better tomorrow. And you didn't. Action coupled with a healthy dose of time is the magic combination.

It took me years to get to where I could openly and without shame tell my story. In brief, here is what it was like and what it's like now:

- At fourteen, I was a heroin addict and a practicing alcoholic; today I'm twenty-six years clean and sober.
- At eighteen, I was a high school dropout who lived homeless on the streets of New York; today I'm a graduate of Georgetown University Law Center and have my own home.
- At twenty-one, I was a prostitute selling my body to support my drug and alcohol habits; today I'm a lawyer, a successful entrepreneur, a loving wife, and a published author.

- At twenty-six, I was hit by a car and told I'd never walk again; in my early forties, I ran two 26.2-mile marathons.
- At twenty-eight, I was the poster child for someone who is selfish, self-centered, and self-absorbed; today, at fifty-two, my life is about being of service to others.

Here are some steps I took that enabled me to get from being traumatized by my past to accepting it, and then being willing to share it with others:

- I came to peace with my history and forgave myself.
- I stopped behaving the way I used to behave. The further away from the old me I got, the easier it was to forgive myself.
- I asked for help. I couldn't do it alone. For some people, therapy might be the answer; for others, a life coach; for still others, just a supportive mentor who has been down the same road.
- I sought out people who had overcome challenges and asked how they did it.
- I recorded my story on paper. There is something to be said for putting pen to paper.
- I started talking about my past to others in a safe environment.
- I recalled times when I was affected by other people's stories. I realized how much they helped me. This made me want to help others by sharing my story.

Telling your story is important for several reasons. There is power in truth-telling because first and foremost it's cathartic. The very act of sharing our life stories with other people lessens our load, particularly if we feel burdened by our past. Sometimes it helps just to get the stuff out. Telling our stories helps us become free from our past. Over the years, as I've had the courage to share my story, my past has less control over me. I'm not so worried that my secret will be discovered, because it's already out!

Here are some other benefits to telling your story:

- You become a role model. You've walked out of the darkness into the light and can now help someone else do the same. I get tons of e-mail from men and women who've struggled with addiction, prostitution, getting through school, failing exams, letting go of destructive relationships, getting married late in life, going for a dream, or just walking through some of life's big and little fears. Hearing my story helps them know anything can be overcome.

- You can see how far you've come. Sharing your story creates a reminder of what happened, what it's like now, and how you got here. This is important in a culture that only celebrates reaching the final destination, not the baby steps along the way. You get to remind yourself of how far you've come.

Everyone has a story. What's yours? This week, you are invited to recount your life and explore the benefits, for yourself, of sharing your story.

DAY 2

When I think about my history, I am reminded that there were several major events that shaped my life. I started drinking and using drugs at fourteen, dropped out of high school at eighteen, got sober at twenty-six, went back to school at twenty-eight, graduated from law school at thirty-three, was admitted to the New York Bar at thirty-seven, got married at forty-five, and published my first book at fifty, just to name a few. To get you thinking about your life story, take some time today and write about your experience up to age fourteen. What do you recall? What, if anything, stands out about that period in your life? Was it a fun time? Were there painful memories? Was there someone in particular who played a significant role? Now let's explore your life through the teen years, fourteen through eighteen. What do you remember? What or who had the most effect on your life during those years?

DAY 3

Now let's move into your later years. Recall your twenties. What were you doing at twenty-one? Twenty-five? Twenty-seven? Is there anything significant about that phase of your life? Does anyone stand out as having played an important role? Are there any particular incidents that shaped your thinking? If you're in your twenties or under, just recall what you can about significant moments in your recent past. What shaped your thinking? What events contributed to who you are today?

DAY 4

If you've lived beyond your twenties, let's explore experiences that had an effect on you at thirty, forty, fifty, and beyond. What do you remember? What had the most impact on your life during those years? Perhaps it was aging. Perhaps you got married or divorced. Maybe you experienced the death of a friend, child, or family pet. Whatever it was, write about the experience and its effect on your life.

DAY 5

Today we're going to bring it all together. Write out your story. You're more ready than you think you are. The hard part has been done; now you just need to bring it together. Chronicle your life, paying particular attention to the events you noted earlier in the week.

DAY 6

Find a friend, a clergy member, or someone else you can share your secrets with. Be selective in your choice. At this stage, *trust* is the operative word. If you're not confident you've found that person, then wait until the right one comes along. One caution: Don't just wait because you're afraid to share. Having the courage to tell the truth will help you more than you can imagine.

DAY 7

Congratulations, you did it! This was a hard week, and you got through it. Good job. Now it's time to rest, recharge, regroup, and review your week. What observations can you make about your behavior his week? What worked? What didn't work? What day seemed extra hard? Why? What did you get from this esteemable acts experience? Now you're ready for the next week.

WEEK 19

Be Silly

Thought for the Week

Self-esteem comes from having the courage
to be playful and silly.

Affirmations for the Week

I am having fun on the journey.

This week, I will allow the kid in me
to come out and play.

Esteemable Actions for the Week

DAY 1

After speaking at a recovery convention, a fellow speaker approached me and said, "Francine, how come you're so serious? You need to lighten up. You never smile. You say you're grateful, but you need to tell your face. You look like it's the end of the world." Well, I thought to myself, "Who does he think he is telling me to lighten up? I'm light. I have a sense of humor, ha ha. I can take a joke—sometimes." As you can imagine, I was just a little peeved. But you know, he was right. After I got down off my high horse, I really got that he was right. I never smile. I'm always serious, and my face looks tense, as if I'm carrying the weight of the world on my shoulders. What's up with that? I hide behind the fact that I am a left-brain thinker and never allow the little girl—the silly person, the humorous person that I believe I really am—to come out and play.

Since that time, I've made a conscious effort to lighten up. The first time I practiced was at a conference where I unhappily forgot what I was talking about. I got conversational with my audience, went off on a tangent, and couldn't remember where I was. In the past when that happened, I was devastated—and you could tell. My hands got sweaty, my body tensed up, and my mouth got dry. I looked scared and I was. But on this particular day, I simply stopped for a minute, took a deep cleansing breath, and blurted out, "Oh my God, I'm having a senior moment." The crowd roared. I didn't die, and I demonstrated that I had a sense of humor about myself. I've been doing it ever since.

I'm still not a "funny" speaker. I don't have my audiences cracking up in their seats, but I've come a long way. I'm willing to laugh, smile, and make light of myself a lot more often. Everything is a process. And I owe much of my progress to my husband. He keeps me laughing at me! There was a time I couldn't cry from the platform, and when I did, I apologized. Not anymore. Now when I cry, I am so grateful I can feel and be real. It's a gift, not an impediment. Now I laugh and cry all in the same talk. Oh my God, what's next?

When we lighten up, we see the world through new eyes. Problems become more manageable. And mistakes aren't the end of our world. We learn to delight in all that God has created, and we become full of joyous expectation of the good that awaits us. Plus, we don't age as quickly because we allow our inner child to come out and play.

What does it take to allow yourself to be silly in the moment? Well, some people are natural humorists. They have the capacity to see something funny in all things, starting with themselves. For many, they have been making people laugh from the time they entered the world. Recall the kids you went to school with who made everybody laugh. They were funny; it was natural for them. But for the rest of us, being silly or lightening up is a learned skill.

In talking to some funny people I know and in using my own learning experience as an example, here is what I've come up with:

- Be willing to look silly. If you're really willing, it'll happen. You must be willing to do the work. Willingness without action is fantasy.

- Identify the beliefs that stand in your way. Some of my unhealthier beliefs were that laughter distracts the audience from the message; that when people laugh they don't have to think, and sometimes thinking is good; that all humor is self-deprecating and offensive; that if you're funny you're not professional and, therefore, not taken seriously.

- Analyze events from your past. Recall a public mistake you made and how you handled it. How would you handle it differently if the situation occurred again?

- Practice making light of yourself. Tell part of your story and inject a little humor.

- Work through any shame that is in the way. The truth is, until I cleaned up my past, I wasn't able to make light of it.

- Practice smiling and keep laughing. It is the best medicine. When you laugh, you look better and feel better. My natural expression is serious, so even today, I catch myself and practice smiling. Of course, this doesn't mean you should smile when it's inappropriate, like at funerals, when someone is hurting, or when someone is sharing a serious story with you.

- Stop being critical of people who have the courage to be silly and make mistakes. When I'm critical of others, I become less willing to put myself on the line for fear of being judged. Bring to mind someone you know who made a mistake in public and got through it. Think of how they handled it, not through critical eyes, but in an effort to learn from them.

- Explore the endless possibilities for being lighthearted and silly. As you go through each day, identify situations where a little humor would change what's happening.
- Don't take yourself so seriously. Life is fun, interesting, challenging, and waiting to happen.

This week, you have permission to get silly. Silliness is an experience of joy. If we are really feeling joyful, then it's to our advantage to show that in all we do.

DAY 2

Bring to mind someone you know who has made a mistake in a public forum and then corrected it in a lighthearted way. For a moment, you might have felt sorry for that person, but afterward, I would imagine you got past what happened, because they did. That person didn't allow a little mistake to get in the way of his or her primary purpose—to connect with his or her audience. What did you learn from this person?

DAY 3

Now think about a mistake you made in public. What happened? How did you feel? Was there anything funny about the situation? Write down two or three ways you would handle that same situation if it occurred again.

DAY 4

Today think about the endless possibilities for being lighthearted and silly. As you go through this day, identify three situations where a little humor would change what's happening.

DAY 5

Practice telling part of your story and inject a little humor. These days, when I talk about wearing hot pants the size of a sash, little blouses that ended at my navel, and leather boots, I laugh because, in truth, it's funny. Boy, was I ever a sight. I make light of it, my audience makes light of it, and I move on.

DAY 6

In *Twelve Steps and Twelve Traditions,* Bill W. spoke of Rule 62: Don't take yourself too seriously. Just keep laughing. It is the best medicine. When you laugh, you look better and feel better.

DAY 7

You did it. You got through another tough week. Good job! Now, on this seventh day, you rest, recharge, regroup, and review your week. What observations can you make about your ability to lighten up and be silly? What worked this week? What didn't? What day seemed extra hard? Why? What did you get from this esteemable acts experience? Now you're ready for the next week.

WEEK

20

Courage to Be Real

Thought for the Week

Self-esteem comes from having the courage
to be real.

Affirmations for the Week

I have the courage to be real.

This week, I will live authentically.

Esteemable Actions for the Week

DAY 1

It is easy to talk about being authentic without having a clue what it really means. Real authenticity refers to the distance between us and other people. And we measure that distance by how willing we are to be real.

There's a constant battle within many of us: "Should I tell the truth or should I look good?" The funny thing is that we think we have a choice. And while we ultimately do, the more aligned we are with our true selves, the less like a choice it feels. Each time you hear a speaker or author use his or her life as a teaching tool, aren't you just a little inspired and in awe? Every time you hear someone tell the truth from the platform, aren't you just a little encouraged to do the same? When a person has the courage to tell the truth, it gives the rest of us permission to do the same.

At a recent convention, two speakers stood out above the rest. One was good; the other was great. At first it was difficult to identify what made one more powerful than the other. Then it hit me. While both shared what it used to be like, what happened, and what it's like now, one created a real connection. The first speaker, whom I'll call Billy, was a good speaker. He knew the Steps, quoted from the Big Book, and had a great sense of humor. But something was missing, and I couldn't quite identify what it was until I experienced Patricia, the second speaker.

Like Billy, Patricia was nicely dressed, articulate, and sober a long time. But when she opened her mouth and started to speak, you knew she expressed a sense of God that took her far beyond good to great. As she talked, I got it! Patricia had a soulful connectedness with the audience that Billy didn't. There was a bond so real that it could only be created by Patricia's willingness to tell the truth and her audience's willingness to receive it.

Both speakers knew the audience, and they both had powerful stories to share, but only Patricia truly shared hers. Billy made us laugh; Patricia made us cry and think. Both were appreciated, but Patricia took us to the level of realness because she was there herself.

Being real takes skill and great courage. Skill, because if done inappropriately, people feel sorry for us—not connected—and we appear to be stuck in the pain of where we are. Or they may perceive us as manipulative—trying to get attention from the group. On the other hand, it takes courage to be real because we risk losing something: face, family, friends, jobs, our reputation for being a certain way. Yet each time we're courageous, it gets easier—not easy, but easier. We become someone people can relate to. And even if our experience differs from theirs in the details, they know we are people who have lived through a fire and can teach them how to do the same.

When first asked to share my story in a public forum, it was frightening, and I was devastated because I hadn't yet made peace with my past. It was hard to admit I was a heroin addict and an alcoholic at fourteen; that I dropped out of high school and lived homeless on the streets at eighteen; that by twenty-one I was a prostitute to support my habits; and that at twenty-six I was so drunk I walked in front of a moving car. Plus, there was still a part of me that saw failure as a fate worse than death, rejection as one of life's bad jokes, and having a colorful past like a scarlet letter embossed upon my forehead—even around people who were like me. In my eyes, being less than perfect was something to be ashamed of, not accepted, and certainly not celebrated. So as I came to terms with my life, as I began to see how my experience was a gift to me, I recognized its utility for others.

This kind of truth-telling makes us approachable and real. In reading these self-disclosing statements, you may be thinking, "She's crazy. How in the world can she disclose such personal information about herself?" Or "How could I ever do something like that?" And maybe part of you says, "Bravo! You go, girl, for having the courage to be authentic. If she can do it, I can do it."

Regardless of what you're thinking, the fact is, you're thinking. And if only a handful of you are inspired to openly talk about your own experience, strength, and hope in an effort to help others, then this week is a success. If only a few of you have the courage to risk going deep into your past, deep into your fear, deep into those places you'd rather forget and use your past as a tool to help others, then what a stunning example of real courage and authenticity you will be.

So how do we move from seeing life as something to be kept secret to using it as an opportunity to serve? How do we move from talking about being authentic to being authentic? Here are some suggestions that helped me and perhaps they will resonate with you:

- Bring to mind someone who had the courage to be real. How did you feel in their presence? Were you able to connect with them in some way? Why?
- Think about a difficulty you faced in your life. What lessons did you learn?
- Share your experience with a trusted friend. Putting words to your past is a first step to being more real over time.
- Listen for opportunities to be real. You may meet someone with a similar problem who needs to know that others share it. If that happens, have the courage to be real and share your experience.
- Keep talking. The more you come clean, the easier it gets—not easy, but easier.
- Come to peace with your past, because the more at peace you are with yourself, the more real you can be.

This week, you are invited to be more real.

DAY 2

Name a person you've encountered who appeared especially real. What made him or her so? Spend a few minutes today writing about that person.

DAY 3

Write about a real-life experience you've had that is sometimes painful to remember. How did it affect you? What lessons did you learn?

DAY 4

Share your feelings about your experience with a trusted friend, someone who won't judge, but will just listen.

DAY 5

Today I invite you to listen for opportunities to be real. There are many people who need to know the pain they feel is not unique to them. Be open to being real with someone who can use a friend today.

DAY 6

Today you're invited to listen for opportunities to help others be real. Many people want to come out of the darkness of their secrets, but they don't know how or don't feel safe doing so. Create a loving space for someone to be real with you.

DAY 7

You did it. You got through another tough week. Good job! Now, on this seventh day, you rest, recharge, regroup, and review your week. What observations can you make about your behavior this week? What worked? What didn't work? What day seemed extra hard? Why? What did you get from this esteemable acts experience? Now you're ready for the next week.

Friendship

Thought for the Week
It's an esteemable act to treasure your friends.

Affirmation for the Week
This week, I will treat my friends
like treasured items.

Esteemable Actions for the Week

DAY 1

Our connection was immediate on our first day at law school. We now have a soulful bond that has spanned almost twenty years. Who would have thought the two of us, from such different worlds, eleven years apart in age, could come together as lifelong friends? Yet we have. She loves animals; so do I. I root for the underdog; so does she. She is an old spirit, wise beyond her years. And when I met her, I had lived a life far beyond my years. Her heart is bristling with love for all things living, and her spirit is quite courageous. That first day of class when Lorraine challenged our contracts professor, I knew we'd be friends. Through career changes, relocations, marriages, disagreements, aging, failed Bar exams, and two law school reunions, we still are friends.

What is friendship? It's a voluntary connection, a bond between two or more people that transcends race, religion, gender, or political persuasion. It's knowing we can count on someone to be there when we need him or her. It's unconditionally being loved, no matter what. It's having someone to laugh with, cry with, dance with, and celebrate with. It's having the courage to tell the truth and having the courage to be told the truth.

Friendship is trusting someone enough to reveal that side of us that we dare not reveal too often. It's knowing a friend will deliver on a promise. It's the offering of whatever we have to give to make our friend's road just a little easier: an ear to listen, a shoulder to cry on, a sofa to crash on, money if needed, our heart, our attention. Friends are like the warm, cozy fire on a cold, damp night. True friendship is a gift from God that we are required to take care of.

How do we get friends? I heard years ago that to have a friend, you must be a friend. For years my mentor Louise reminded me that as long as I found it necessary to sleep with other women's husbands, I wouldn't have any girlfriends. What a novel concept. Yet the truth is, at that time in my life I didn't think I needed women in my life. "Women are too competitive," I'd say. "They can't be trusted. They back stab you." Of course, I knew that was true because I helped to perpetuate such beliefs by my own behavior. Today I know the value and ultimate utility of same-sex friendships.

Where do we find friends? Everywhere we are: the hallway in our apartment building, our job, the elevator, the gym, the opera, in church, at a community meeting, at PTA. Wherever we show up, there are opportunities to make friends. Some friends pass through our lives on a temporary mission. Others stay for a while, perhaps months or even years. Their charge is to assist us along the journey in a way that only they can do. Their expertise is needed at that moment in time. But then there are those who come for the long haul. They share our journey in a special way, and a slice of history is created.

What gets in the way of friendship? Hurt feelings, ego, family, other friends, work, other commitments, changing values, changing goals, and distance. And some relationships, seemingly through nobody's fault, just fade away. Yet I believe that no relationship just dies. Like anything else, where we place our attention is what gets fed and grows. If a relationship reaches its expiration, it's because we have allowed that to happen for some reason.

This week, you're invited to think about the people you have at some time or another called friends. We'll explore what you appreciate about them and ways you can let them know, and if appropriate, how you can reconnect with them.

DAY 2

In your own words, define friendship. To help you, bring to mind someone you consider—or have ever considered—to be a friend. List the characteristics that make him or her a good friend. What things do you have in common? What makes the relationship work?

DAY 3

Today make a list of your closest friends. It doesn't matter whether they live in your neighborhood, your state, or clear across the globe. When you think of your real friends, who comes to mind? Why?

DAY 4

Think of someone you listed on day 3 and bring to mind an experience you had with your friend that made you know he or she was on your team. Really allow yourself to recall that time in your life. What happened? How did you feel? How did the experience bring you closer together?

DAY 5

Contact the people on your list. Make a call, send a thank-you note, or send a card saying "Just thinking of you" to them. This is your day to appreciate the people who have been there as friends. In some cases, it simply might be an opportunity to reconnect. Whatever the reason to say hello, don't let this day go by without making contact with your friends.

DAY 6

Identify two people who are currently out of your life, but who at one time were important. What happened? Use today to reflect on times past, when there was love between you. Even though much time may have passed, if appropriate, I invite you to make a call, send an e-mail, or write a note saying, "Hi, it has been a long time. I'm thinking about you."

DAY 7

Today is your Four Rs Day, time once again for you to rest, recharge, regroup, and review your week. What observations can you make about your behavior his week? What worked? What didn't work? What day seemed extra hard? Why? For some of you, this day will seem just a little more challenging than those that came before. Nonetheless, I urge you to take this day to practice the four Rs.

Let Go of Victimhood

Thought for the Week

Self-esteem comes from letting go of victimhood.

Affirmations for the Week

I am not a victim.

This week, I will make different choices.

Esteemable Actions for the Week

DAY 1

The unabridged version of the *Random House Dictionary of the English Language* defines *victim* as "a person who suffers from a destructive or injurious action or agency . . . a person who is deceived or cheated . . . *a victim of misplaced confidence.*" Based on this definition, to some degree or another, we've all been victims. We've all suffered at the hands of a cruel or misguided person, whether the action was intentional or not. Perhaps it was a parent, a teacher, a member of the clergy, a sibling or other member of our family, or just someone who was close to us. Maybe the suffering was because we grew up poor, were confined to an institution, or were disabled. Or maybe some past experience affected us so much that we became emotionally impotent. In life, we sometimes get a bad break or many bad breaks. What we do with these bad breaks makes the difference in the lives we ultimately live.

For years I saw myself as a victim. And I believed I was justified. "If you had my life," I'd moan, "you'd behave the same way, too." As I saw it, being black, being born into poverty, having had a history of drug addiction and alcoholism, and having had a series of bad relationships gave me a ready-made excuse to feel sorry for myself. And I milked that attitude all I could, for as long as I could, until the day came when it just no longer worked for me.

While I'd like to say I no longer see myself as a victim, in truth, daily I fight the tendency to hold on to my old ideas. For example, the other day I was sitting in traffic on the freeway and someone cut me off. My initial urge was to give him the finger and shout expletives from my car window. But instead, I honored my second thought and did nothing. I chose the high road. It has taken years of work for the second thought to become my reality. There was a time when I would have shouted horrible words, then blamed the other person for my behavior: I was a victim of circumstances; had they not done what they did, I would not have done what I did; it wasn't my fault; they made me do it; and so on.

It's hard to shift from a mode of thinking we've relied on for so long. A manner of thinking that serves us in countless ways. Even though the benefits of letting go of the victim mentality outweigh the negatives, there are far too many payoffs that keep us chained to the "it's not my fault" or "poor me" frame of mind. Here are a few benefits of being a victim. Some render seemingly big payoffs:

- Victims always have someone to blame. When things go wrong, no matter what part you play, if you're a victim and the outcome is negative, it's never your fault.
- As a victim you have permission to be depressed, and most people will not care enough to expect you to "get on with it."

- You'll never be expected to rise above your beginnings and make something of yourself.
- You won't be encouraged to "let go and let God" regarding your past, because you just can't do it.
- No one will ever say, "Get off that couch and stop taking drugs, drinking booze, and eating bon bons." And if they do, you'll have one more reason to feel victimized: "Poor me. They just don't understand."
- You're in good company. There are far more people seeing themselves as victims than who are taking responsibility for their choices. You'll always fit in with the majority.
- As a victim you have permission to wait for others to change, and if they don't (and they probably won't), you have an excuse to do nothing.

Yes, indeed, there are many benefits to holding on to the victim consciousness. But there are also benefits to being responsible for your life:

- You get results.
- You complete tasks.
- You feel a sense of freedom.
- You are in control of your life and your destiny.
- You have choices.
- Your life is full of endless possibilities.
- You view obstacles as opportunities.
- You are happier.
- You feel more vital.

The cycle of victimhood is hard to break, because it's safe, it's familiar, and it requires little effort to sustain. As a result, it takes willingness, a real willingness to walk through the fear that stands between self-empowerment and a victim consciousness. How do we break the cycle? How do we get past victimhood to empowerment?

How do we move out of the darkness into the light? How can we create a different experience for ourselves? Here are a few actions—esteemable actions—to consider:

- Make a decision to take back your life. I got sick and tired of being sick and tired and of having no control over my life. It was a hard decision to make because with choice comes responsibility. But it has been worth the effort.
- Identify areas where you feel out of control or lacking power. Is it your job that feels out of control, your money, your family situation? Whatever it is, having the courage to admit it is a step toward taking back your life.
- Think through your choices before making a final decision. Poor choices are often a setup for feeling like a victim. I jumped into relationships with very unhealthy men over and over again. The signs were there: they were already married, they had a roving eye, they had a drinking problem, they didn't have a job, they yelled at me and called me names. Then when they did what they were destined to do, because the signs were there, I cried, "Poor me. Look at what he did to me."
- Feel your feelings and walk through your fear. No one said it was going to be easy, but having the courage to walk through your fear is a first step toward freedom. It's better to feel a little uncomfortable because you said no rather than feel the pain of having to clean up the mess you made because you were afraid to say no early in the game.
- Get help. It's hard to hold yourself accountable. Every time I blame someone, my accountability buddy asks, "What part did you play?"

This week, you are invited to focus on letting go of victimhood.

DAY 2

Today is the day you make a decision to stop being a victim. It's easier said than done, but doable. Bring to mind all the times you have been at the mercy of someone else, all the times your feelings have felt like a basketball, bouncing all around from one side of the court to another. List all the times you've given your power away to someone, only to walk away feeling very miserable and drained. Today you're simply invited to make a decision to take back your life. Create your intention.

DAY 3

Using yesterday's list and your intention to stop being a victim, get into the solution today. What one action can you take that moves you into the solution?

DAY 4

One of the quickest ways to shift from victim to empowered person is by making different and healthier choices. You do that by thinking through your process before you make a final decision. You do it by having the courage to ask questions for clarification and by keeping your eyes and ears open. You do it by thinking through the consequences of your actions. What three actions can you take today that will help you feel more empowered?

DAY 5

Feel your feelings and do it anyway. Walking through fear is the single best antidote for a scary situation. People are always asking me, "Francine, how do you walk through the fear?" And my response is always, "By taking one baby step at a time." So I ask you, what feelings surfaced as you walked through your fear and did yesterday's assignment? Share that experience with a trusted friend.

DAY 6

Today you may find you still are not as connected as you'd like to be. Consider getting help. In this age of community and fellowship, why not have the courage to reach out for support?

DAY 7

Today is your Four Rs Day, time once again for you to rest, recharge, regroup, and review your week. What observations can you make about your behavior this week? What worked? What didn't work? What day seemed extra hard? Why? For some of you, this day will seem just a little more challenging than those that came before. Nonetheless, I urge you to take this day to practice the four Rs.

WEEK 23

Do the Right Thing, Now

Thought for the Week

It's an esteemable act to do the right thing
in the moment.

Affirmations for the Week

I am responsible for creating my second chance.

This week, I will learn from my missed
opportunities.

Esteemable Actions for the Week

DAY 1

Have you ever done something you later regretted, but then found it was too late to make it right? Have you ever wished you had just one more chance to make an amend for harm done? One more opportunity to right a wrong? Often in life we are given second chances, opportunities to rectify situations with outcomes we don't like. Perhaps we let a relationship die because we were too proud to admit we were wrong. Or we let it expire because we weren't able to forgive when the wrong was done to us. Sometimes we have a chance to make right those painful situations and live in harmony with those we once vowed never to talk to again. And sometimes we don't.

Sometimes we simply miss the opportunity to make amends, to say "I'm sorry" or "I love you" or to forgive. And when we miss those opportunities, regardless of how many people tell us "You're fine" and "It's not your fault," in our heart of hearts, we know there is something more we could have done. No amount of "let go and let God" will erase the pain that we are left with when we've truly missed an opportunity. I learned the hard way the importance of resolving unfinished business before it's too late.

The call came at 5:30 a.m. No longer did I have to worry about whether I should call and make up, whether the argument had been my fault, or whether she was to blame for being more controlling and unreasonable than I was. It no longer mattered who was right or who started the argument. I didn't have to worry anymore because she was dead. As of that moment, the problem was moot, buried with her. Or was it? In truth, something died inside me too. The last time we argued, I remember saying to myself about Penny, "I wish she were dead." And now she was. Not that I in any way caused her death, but because of the unfinished business between us, her memory will always live within me as an opportunity missed.

Upon hearing the news, all I could think was, "I wish I had one more chance to do the right thing and say 'I'm sorry.'" But there were no more chances, no more opportunities. Yet it didn't have to be that way. I could have done it differently had I been willing to get past my feelings and walk through my fear.

Some people might say, "Don't be so hard on yourself. You did the best you could at the time. It wasn't your fault, Francine." And while that soothes my grieving, aching heart in the moment, it doesn't exonerate me from my actions. I know there was more I could have done. So how do we avoid being in this place of sadness and guilt? We walk through the fear and take right action when we have the chance.

What prevents us from doing what's needed in the moment? An assortment of old ideas: we believe we're right, we hurt from a past transgression, we think someone else is to blame, we fear what people will think if we initiate a conciliatory action, we're unable or unwilling to forgive, we don't know how to forgive, or we don't know how to admit we're wrong. Whatever our reason, not doing what's needed in the moment can lead to missed opportunities. And while our reasons may be valid in the moment, there we sit with an ache in our heart and a memory that impedes our serenity.

Is it really worth the effort? Is it more important to be right than comfortable? Perhaps for some of us it is. Perhaps for some it's a matter of principle. The esteemable acts process invites you to get past the problem to the solution, if not for the sake of others, then for your own sake. We never know how long we have to live. Making the very best of each moment is a gift we give to ourselves.

Sometimes the missed opportunities are not about people at all, but about opportunities in life. Have you ever had a job or the occasion to collaborate on a project, but your attitude ruined the deal? My most notable display of bad attitude happened in my second year of law school. I accepted a terrific summer associate job at a prestigious midsize New York law firm. I was smart; I could adapt. I was passionate about the law. But sometimes all the skill in the world can't and won't overcome a bad attitude. Instead of trying to work with other summer associates, I created barriers because I felt I was better than them. I was older, so I thought I was more mature. I didn't drink, so I thought I was classier. I was working my way through school, so I thought I deserved a position more than they did. I was at Georgetown, so I thought I was "Ms. It." Each action I took created a greater wedge between us, until my attitude became a topic of constant discussion. Upon completing law school, every summer associate was invited back to work at this firm—every associate but me.

Years after the experience, I continued to blame the firm, citing reasons such as prejudice, jealousy, that I wasn't a party girl, and that I am a woman. The truth is I blew it. I missed the opportunity to practice law at a wonderful firm. I let my fear of fitting in create unnecessary barriers for me. Sometimes life is unfair due to no fault of our own. And sometimes life is hard because of the choices we make. The wisdom to know the difference is the key to not missing the opportunities.

This week, you're invited to examine your life for missed opportunities and identify potential ones that can be averted now.

DAY 2

Bring to mind a missed opportunity in your life—an experience that, had you been willing to walk through your fear and take an action, might have turned out differently. What were the circumstances surrounding that opportunity? Who was involved? Write about it today.

DAY 3

Rarely does a life experience go by without some learning attached. Keeping in mind the missed opportunity from day 2, what lessons have you learned? What could you have done differently? What part, if any, did you play in what occurred? How could you avoid repeating the same situation?

DAY 4

Recall a situation that you handled differently, one in which you made a different choice and your outcome was more to your liking. Write about it today.

DAY 5

Today you're invited to go deep inside yourself and identify a potential missed opportunity. Is there unfinished business for you to tend to today? For some of you, this will be an opportunity to bring closure to something you need to address. Is there a parent or friend you haven't spoken to for years? Maybe you need to make amends.

Maybe you're in a situation where there is still time to change your attitude or your behavior, like being on probation at work. What part, if any, is your responsibility? How can you avoid this becoming a missed opportunity? What one small action can you take today?

DAY 6

Is there another missed opportunity you can address today? Why not do it? Make a list of actions you can take to clean up unfinished business. Resolving these issues gives you the chance to grow spiritually and, at the same time, genuinely improve your self-esteem.

DAY 7

Today is your Four Rs Day, time once again for you to rest, recharge, regroup, and review your week. What observations can you make about your behavior this week? What worked? What didn't work? What day seemed extra hard? Why? For some of you, this day will seem just a little more challenging than those that came before. Nonetheless, I urge you to take this day to practice the four Rs.

Don't Judge a Book by Its Cover

Thought for the Week

It's an esteemable act not to judge a book
by its cover.

Affirmations for the Week

I make an effort to acknowledge what I have
in common with others.

This week, I will practice not rushing
to judgment.

Esteemable Actions for the Week

DAY 1

On the plane to Hawaii, I sat next to a man wearing a knit skullcap, sweatsuit, sneakers, and dark glasses. As I do whenever someone sits next to me, I said hello. But then I immediately thought, "He must be one of those hip-hoppers." And because of my innate belief about hip-hoppers, I formed an opinion that was negative. I assumed he wasn't smart, was into drugs, and was denigrating toward women. So, while courteous, I had nothing more to say.

There was silence, except when I expressed the obligatory "Excuse me" when I passed him to go to the lavatory. Then, ninety minutes into the flight, the attendant offered dessert and an after-dinner drink. He surveyed his choices: hot fudge sundae, cheesecake, or amaretto. Laughingly he said, "I'll pass, thanks, I'm on my way to work." I thought, "On his way to work from San Francisco to Hawaii, and no cheesecake or sundae? What could he be doing?" Curious as to what he meant, I asked, "What do you do for a living?"

"I'm a mariner," he said.

"What's that?" I asked.

For the next thirty minutes, I was fascinated. His stories of living on the water for four months at a time were geographical history lessons. As I listened, in the back of my mind I was embarrassed at how I had prejudged him. Then I thought to myself, "How often do I do that? How often do I make assumptions about people based on the way they look, how they dress, the car they drive, where they live, who they love, where they went to school, the color of their skin, their familial associations, or their religious choices?"

As I thought about it, I realized I do it way too often. Without even being conscious of my behavior, much of my day is spent judging others. Why? Because there is a payoff, and in my mind, it's worth it. When I'm judging other people, it feeds into an existing belief I have about myself: that I'm better than you or worse than you. And either way, I come up the loser. Also, when I'm judging others, I don't have to look at myself. The focus is on what they're doing, not what I'm doing. Finally, it supports my thinking that I can't possibly have anything in common with people I perceive as different, because I'm not like them. What a great way to keep my world small. How often do you prejudge others?

With all the supposed benefits of judgment, if you're like me, there's also a price to pay. Your thinking essentially makes you a bigot. Your pool of available friendships is limited. Your client base and your team of business associates are narrowed. Your knowledge is inadequate because your source of information is restricted to only those who think like you. Finally, judgment makes you angry, and anger is unattractive because it eats away at your spirit.

So what about you? How often do you rush to judgment? Your initial response may be to say, "Never, I'm open-minded. Everyone is equal." But I invite you to go beyond the rhetoric and really examine your beliefs, assumptions, and behaviors about people you perceive as different. This week, you'll be given that chance.

DAY 2

In this twenty-four hours, I invite you to be aware of how many times you prejudge people you come in contact with. Just pay attention to how often you look at someone and then form a negative opinion about him or her without having all the facts. Every time you catch yourself judging someone, make a note of it.

DAY 3

Today bring to mind one specific situation in the last seven days where you prejudged someone. What triggered your judgment? Was it the clothes he or she wore or didn't wear? Was his or her style too formal? Too casual? Too provocative? Was he or she too assertive? Too passive? Was he or she disabled? Did he or she speak another language? Did he or she not share your political views? Was he or she overweight? Was his or her hair color different than yours? Was he or she pierced in places you don't think should be pierced? Was he or she of a different race or culture? Did he or she have more or less education than you? Did he or she drive a fancier car or no car at all? Was he or she intimate with someone of a different race? There are many ways to judge.

DAY 4

Is judgment of others a repetitive behavior for you? If so, one way to stop such conduct is to understand why you do it. Likely your reason is tied to some perceived benefit. Think back on the situations from day 2 or 3. What benefit did you gain from prejudging the person you spoke of? How did you feel, particularly if you shared your feelings or opinions with others? Sometimes there's a false sense of self when we think or talk badly about others.

DAY 5

Today let's get into the solution. What can you do to be less judgmental? For one thing, you'll be less likely to rush to judgment if you see something in others you relate to or if, for a moment, you are able to put yourself in his or her shoes. Today you're invited to find one thing you have in common with each person you encounter. This may take a little extra work, but the payoff is great. I know you can do it.

DAY 6

Today continue to be aware of your reactions toward others, particularly how quickly you form negative opinions. Continue to acknowledge at least one similarity between you and each person you come in contact with.

DAY 7

You're once again at day 7, your day to rest, recharge, regroup, and review. What observations can you make about your behavior this week? Was the idea of suspending judgment problematic? What worked for you? What didn't? Was one day harder than the others?

WEEK 25

Get Up, Dust Yourself Off, and Start All Over Again

Thought for the Week

Self-esteem comes from not letting obstacles
get you down.

Affirmations for the Week

I am not stopped by life's obstacles.

This week, I will learn from my failures and
mistakes and keep on going.

Esteemable Actions for the Week

DAY 1

Obstacles can materialize in many different ways. The appearance
of a pink slip from your employer when your goal is to get promoted. A rejection letter from a literary agent when your goal is to
get published. Divorce papers when you saw yourself living happily
ever after with the man or woman of your dreams. A series of road-
blocks when you are trying to finish a project or reach a goal.

Recently I was trying to get into San Francisco for a meeting at
noon. On a good day, the drive takes about twenty minutes, but
during rush hour or when it's raining, it easily takes an hour. To be
safe, I gave myself an hour and a half to get to the financial district,

park my car, and comfortably arrive at my destination. And I even took reading material just in case I had time to spare. On this day, for some reason, the traffic going south on 101 was unusually backed up, all the way into Sausalito. As I sat in the same spot for twenty-five minutes, two things occurred to me: (1) I was happy I gave myself extra time and (2) there was something else I could do in the face of this obstacle. In the past, I would have been so freaked out that I couldn't think straight. Today I felt in control of my mind, even if I had no control over my situation.

Inch by inch, as I approached the last exit before the Golden Gate Bridge, I decided to turn around, go north on 101 to the Richmond Bridge, and take the East Bay into San Francisco. With that new strategy, it took me exactly fifty-five minutes to reach my destination. I walked into my meeting with five minutes to spare. While I wished I had had more time to settle in, the fact is I wasn't late. I met my goal of getting to my appointment on time, despite the obstacles in the way. Obstacles that could have ruined my day. I could have continued to sit in traffic, complained about how unfair the situation was, and gotten myself sick with anger. Instead, because I had some extra time, I was able to think of options that allowed me to get around the problem to a solution that worked.

Obstacles are a part of life. They are *perceived* barriers to reaching a goal, completing a task, or satisfying a dream. They happen when we least expect them, and they often take on lives of their own—when we let them.

There are big payoffs to being stuck in a problem, benefits to allowing hurdles in our lives to become the focal point. We feel justified in feeling like a victim, we can get sympathy, we can give up without making a good-faith effort, and we have an excuse to avoid dealing with the challenges in life.

However, there is a greater return on our investment when we have the courage to walk through our discomfort and face our challenges head on. When we don't let them wear us down and force us to give up, we ultimately reach our destination—perhaps a little shaken, a little weathered, and sometimes a little late—but we get there. The more we practice facing challenges, the easier the process becomes. While it's never really easy to overcome obstacles, because we've done it before, we know we can do it again. We gain real self-esteem because we stretch beyond our comfort zone in ways we never thought possible to discover a solution to the seemingly impossible.

It's easy to do what's easy. It's easy to be happy, joyous, and free when life is free of challenges and complications. It's easy to follow our dreams when every tool is readily available. But overcoming life's difficulties often makes us emotionally, mentally, and sometimes physically stronger.

Below are some suggestions to help you get over the hurdles:

- When possible, give yourself plenty of time to deal with the potential obstacles. When the pressure of time is removed or lessened, you can think through your options.
- Know you won't die. Sometimes it seems that you'll never get past the difficult situation. This too shall pass.
- Don't resort to blaming. Blaming others keeps you stuck and unable to focus on solutions. Furthermore, you often play a part in what happens to you.
- Keep the end in mind. When the road gets a little bumpy, you'll want to give up. Don't. Keep your end in mind. What are you trying to accomplish? Where are you headed? What's your ultimate goal?
- Ask yourself, "What can I learn from this experience?" Obstacles provide us with great learning opportunities.
- Ask for help and be open to a new and different strategy. When it comes to your own issues, you may be myopic, able only to see what you want to see. Sometimes it takes an objective person to help you see what went wrong or what you can do to get out of the

uncomfortable situation. Regarding my example of driving into San Francisco, I called my husband while I was sitting in traffic, and it was his suggestion that I take a different route.

- Talk about your feelings with others. The act of sharing helps you know you are not alone, removes the sting, and enables you to help others who might be suffering in silence.
- Don't let a failure or rejection or mistake stop you in your tracks. Depending on the situation, you may have to try again. Remember your goal. You can try again—maybe not tomorrow, but sometime.
- Let go temporarily. Depending on how consumed you are, you might need to let go and rest, recharge, regroup, and review your strategy.

This week, you're invited to explore how you've handled obstacles in the past and, in moving forward, take the opportunity to make some different choices.

DAY 2

Bring to mind a time when you set out to accomplish a task or reach a goal, only to be faced with a seemingly insurmountable obstacle. A time when it seemed that the universe was conspiring against you. A time when you sacrificed everything for a dream and it didn't turn out as you planned. What are the details of your experience? Perhaps it was something you've resolved or perhaps it's still pending. Recall the details of the experience. Did you blame, lose focus, or get so mad you couldn't see other alternatives?

DAY 3

Think back on the situation from day 2. If you ultimately reached your goal, what did it take? What tools did you use to get around the obstacle? If you didn't, what lessons did you learn? What could you have done differently?

DAY 4

To keep your focus on your destination and not on the obstacles, bring to mind a success you've had in the past, particularly when you overcame a problem. How did you succeed? What actions did you take? Shine a light on those times you successfully overcame an obstacle. Success leaves clues.

DAY 5

Learning to be open to feedback is the most important way I've been able to overcome obstacles. Whether it was dealing with my past mistakes and failures or a challenge in my present, being willing to take suggestions has helped me reach my goals. Using either your example from day 2 or a new example, think of someone who could give you honest, thoughtful feedback. Consider someone who has experienced a similar situation, or someone who loves you enough to honestly share his or her opinion. Be aware that your tendency may be to get defensive and reject any suggestion that appears critical. I urge you to be open to the constructive feedback. Today ask that person to help you.

DAY 6

Talk about your feelings. Start with people you feel are safe, such as your therapist, your spiritual leader, or anyone you can trust. Then gradually step outside your comfort zone and share with others who will listen. Often we're reluctant to speak about what happened because we fear we'll be judged, we'll be misunderstood, or people will tire of our story. So what if they judge you! You won't die. Self-esteem comes from walking through the fear of what people will think. In the long run, you'll be stronger and healthier for the experience.

When I failed the Bar exam, everyone knew it. Failing was hard and so was talking about it. I was embarrassed, but at the wise suggestion of my mentor Louise, I continued to walk through my fear of being judged and told the truth about the experience. The more I talked about it, the less painful it was. Today one of my greatest strengths is my willingness to deal with obstacles and talk about my experience.

DAY 7

Here we are at day 7, and once again you're invited to rest, recharge, regroup, and review your week. Was it hard to relive painful failures, rejections, and mistakes? How did you feel when you succeeded? If you didn't, when will you try again? What did you learn about yourself? What observations can you make about your behavior this week? What worked for you? What didn't?

WEEK 26

What Does It Really Mean?

Thought for the Week

It's an esteemable act to stop and smell the roses.

Affirmations for the Week

I take time to understand what I learn.

This week, I will practice digesting what I learn.

Esteemable Actions for the Week

DAY 1

For years I diligently and faithfully read my daily meditations. I worked them into my routine activities, just as I shower, brush my teeth, and press my clothes. After each reading, I'd stop and digest the material, allowing myself to mentally interpret each passage's meaning. It was a great way to begin my day. But over the years, I became careless in my reading and rushed through my daily meditations. As a result, I missed the essence of what keeps me grounded.

Do you really take the time to understand the meaning of your daily readings? On average, I'd imagine too few of us do. When we skim through our readings, we miss the real benefit of these powerful, inspirational, mind-altering tools. There is a richness in our reading that has the power to change a day, avert a disaster, calm a nerve, or untwist a mind wrought with anger. Think of how often a few words from a favorite book have turned around a bad day. Think of how often you were stuck on a point or confused by a feeling, and reading just the right words from a daily guide provided comfort and clarity. Think of a time when you needed help in making sense of an experience and you opened your book to just the right page, seemingly by accident. When we don't process what we read, how can it help us?

Why don't we take time to really absorb what we read? We're in a hurry and just don't have the time for the *seemingly* unimportant. Also, there is work involved in reading—we must interact with the material. It's an active, participatory process. If there is something we don't understand, it's our responsibility to work through it, look up words in the dictionary, or ask for help.

Yet if we invest the time, we will experience more abundance and a greater sense of serenity. We'll discover tools for living that previously eluded us. We'll feel better equipped to handle situations that used to baffle us because we're participating in our solution. We'll know a new freedom and a new happiness because we'll know we are not alone.

This week, you're invited to take time to read, understand, and really digest your daily inspirational readings. You'll be given six distinct opportunities to do so. The more you practice reading for understanding, the easier it becomes and the more you will benefit.

DAY 2

Select one meditation from any source that appeals to you. It could be a book of daily meditations such as *Each Day a New Beginning* or *Touchstones*. You might want to read a book of inspirational stories such as those from the Chicken Soup for the Soul series. It could be a section from any of your favorite books that touch your heart and aid in shifting your consciousness. It could be the Bible or the Big Book or anything in between. Today your task is simply to open a book, digest what you read, write a short paragraph about what the reading means to you, and ask yourself, "How does it apply to me?"

DAY 3

Today select another reading and repeat the process: read, digest what you read, write a short paragraph about the reading, and ask yourself, "How does it apply to me?"

DAY 4

Today select a different reading and repeat the process: read, digest what you read, write a short paragraph about the reading, and ask yourself, "How does it apply to me?"

DAY 5

Today select another reading and repeat the process: read, digest what you read, write a short paragraph about the reading, and ask yourself, "How does it apply to me?"

DAY 6

Today select one more reading and repeat the process: read, digest what you read, write a short paragraph about the reading, and ask yourself, "How does it apply to me?" By the end of today you should be in the habit of really reading for understanding.

DAY 7

Here we are at day 7. Once again you're invited to rest, recharge, regroup, and review your week. Was it hard to read material and really take time to apply your learning? What observations can you make about your behavior this week? What worked for you? What didn't? Did the assignments get easier?

Reassess Your Year

Thought for the Week

It's an esteemable act to do a periodic check-in
regarding your goals.

Affirmations for the Week

I am reassessing my goals.

This week, I am willing to do a midyear check-in.

Esteemable Actions for the Week

DAY 1

Here you are, at the midpoint in your year. Have you followed
through on the early goals you set for yourself? Are you on track
with the actions you need to take this month? Have you made a
daily effort to do just one little thing that moves you closer to your
dream? Are things going along fine or is it time to tweak your position? A midyear review allows you to evaluate your results and modify wherever appropriate.

All successful businesses take stock of their inventory, their assets, and their liabilities. They look at first and second quarterly
earnings and assess what's working and what's not. They examine
their strategy to determine whether something needs changing. Why

should we, as people striving to be more successful in our personal lives, be any different? In fact, taking stock of where we are is not only good business sense but also spiritually sound. Doing it mid-way allows us to see how far we've come and make any necessary adjustments to our plan of action.

Some of you are exactly where you want to be and feel the benefits of positive, self-directed, consistent action. For you, the year is a productive exercise in moving toward a stated goal. You're excited and motivated. Even if there are days when you skip a beat, you're willing to get back on track. You know you'll succeed, because you're willing to stay the course.

Others of you, while not exactly where you want to be, are only slightly behind in your schedule. You've steadily been doing the work. You've followed through on your weekly and monthly goals while focusing on the ultimate prize. Your position is strong, and if you continue with your work, you'll see results.

Then there are some of you who will look at your goals and feel you've made no progress. For whatever reason, you're not where you want to be. Perhaps you were too busy, maybe you had too much on your plate, perhaps other people's emergencies became yours, maybe you just decided you didn't want to do any work, maybe fear reared its ugly little head and said, "Why even bother?" Whatever the reason, don't be discouraged if you haven't accomplished all you wanted to by this point. Feel the feelings. Take an hour and feel sorry for yourself if you need to. Then get on with it. Spending too much time in a regretful mode is not productive. It slows you down and keeps you focused on what isn't, instead of what can be. As an alternative, acknowledge what you have done and reassess your position. Now is the time to create a plan for moving forward, so you can make your goals for this year a reality. The good news is that the year isn't over. There is still plenty of time to make changes—if you want. The key is to identify the necessary changes and then be willing to do the work. Maybe you need to do a little more of something, or a little bit less, or revamp the plan altogether. Whatever you decide, you still have a solid six months to implement the change.

You can do it. Let's start by answering the following questions:

1. What was your goal for the year? Bring your goal back into your consciousness. Sometimes all it takes is remembering what's important and what's not.

2. Did you define your goal as a SWARM goal (see pages 41–42)? Was it specific, written down somewhere, achievable, realistic, and measurable?

3. In looking back over the last six months, what got in your way? Why are you not further along on your path? What do you think stops you?

4. There are always positive things to acknowledge. What did you do well? What worked for you?

5. What didn't work during the last six months? Were you not prepared for the obstacles? Did you try to tackle too many things at once?

6. Did you forget about the baby steps? Baby steps are a critical part of realizing a dream. Did you get so excited that you started taking big steps, then took on too much and gave up altogether?

7. Do you have a visual reminder? If so, what is it? Do you look at it often? Rarely? Not at all? If you don't have a visual reminder, why not? What can you use to keep yourself focused during the remaining six months?

8. Did you stay connected to a buddy or have a coach to support your effort, or did you try to do it alone?

A benefit of periodically assessing yourself is that you can always make a change. There is plenty of time. Making a start is the key.

This week, let's assess where you are. If you're on track, keep up the good work and continue to do what you're doing. Use this week to recommit. If you're slightly off track, I'm here to help you jump back on the horse and start riding.

DAY 2

Today let's remember your goal. What is it? What was important to you at the beginning of the year? Write each goal down on a colored index card. Make the commitment to make it real. Ask yourself, "Is it still achievable and realistic?" If it's still achievable but less realistic over six months, modify it to accommodate your time frame. Do something rather than nothing. For example, suppose your goal is to lose fifty pounds. That might have been more doable during twelve months. So why not revise your goal to lose twenty-five pounds or ten pounds in six months? It's a start.

DAY 3

In looking back over the last six months, what got in your way? What prevented you from doing more? What didn't work over the last six months? Were you not prepared for the obstacles? Did you try to tackle too many things at once? Did you forget about the baby steps? Write out your answers. There is a power in putting pen to paper and looking at your thought process.

DAY 4

Rarely does a day go by when we don't do something positive. Today bring to mind some positive actions you took over the last six months. What did you do well? What worked for you?

DAY 5

Do you have a visual reminder? If so, what is it? Do you look at it often? Rarely? Not at all? If you don't have a visual reminder, why not? What can you use to stay focused over the remaining six months? Today create a visual reminder of your goal. Then keep it visible everywhere you are.

DAY 6

Utilizing a support system is key. Did you stay connected to a buddy? What about a mastermind group, several people in your support system with whom you meet weekly or monthly? Mastermind groups are a great way for people with the common purpose of supporting one another to help each other get to the next level. Have you considered working with a coach? Today is your day to commit to securing some kind of support.

DAY 7

Today you're invited to rest, recharge, regroup, and review your week. What observations can you make about your ability to honestly assess your position? Was it helpful to have a midyear check-in? Is there anything else that may stop you from doing the work required to get you to the end of the year?

You Are the Artist in Your Life

Thought for the Week

It's an esteemable act to create the life you want.

Affirmations for the Week

I create the life I want.

This week, I will practice being the artist
in my life.

Esteemable Actions for the Week

DAY 1

You are the artist in your life. You create the images and colors on
the canvas called your life. Are you creating the picture you want?
Does your canvas convey a life of fulfillment and growth? Or does
your canvas convey chaos and despair?

Sometimes we don't like what we see in our lives. And I ask,
"Who is responsible for the likeness reflecting back?" Some would
say outside forces, such as inadequate parents, poverty, addiction,
rotten breaks, racism, homophobia, a disability, incest, and any
number of other things. No doubt, outside forces can and do influ-
ence our life canvas. But I invite you to consider that, more often
than not, we allow outside forces to color and define our lives.

You are the artist; God is your co-creator. Together all things are possible. But when we mistakenly believe that other people control our destiny, we end up feeling bitter and hopeless. In truth, we're in partnership with a Higher Power, or whatever you choose to call it. I call that power God. We make the initial decisions; God carries out our plans. God could not render our lives what they are without our assistance. We are the artists, and ultimately we call the shots.

For years that was hard for me to accept. My life was rotten. I had a drug habit and an addiction to alcohol, I was selling my body to support my dysfunctional lifestyle, and I was making bad choices that led to more bad choices. And I thought it wasn't my fault. I wasn't the artist who created this mess. I remember thinking, "If only I had a break, if only someone would give me a chance, my life would be different." Sadly, when a few kindly folks tried to give me breaks, I blew the opportunities.

How easy it is to believe we have no control over the events of our lives. How easy it is to believe our lives are preordained and that someone has control over the details. Holding on to that belief renders a big payoff, because when things go wrong, it's not our fault. And when things go right, it was just God's will. But never do we play a part. Or so we think.

This week, I invite you to consider a different perspective. This may not be easy to swallow if you are a struggling single parent, someone who has just lost a job, or someone facing other tough circumstances. You're invited to first see whether you played a part in where you are. And the best news you can give yourself is to say yes, because if you played even a small part, there is something you can do to change that canvas of your life. But if you played no part whatsoever, then you may be waiting forever for someone to change the course of your life. And that could be a very long wait. Even if you played no part, what can you do today to re-create your life? What action can you take to create a more appealing image? You are the artist in your life.

This week, we'll focus on both your work and home environments, your image, and your relationships. What picture are you creating this week and how can you make it better? And money's not an object. There are little things you can do to beautify yourself, your living space, and your work space. There are also small changes you can make regarding the people in your life. You're invited to be your own artist this week. And you have at your fingertips all the necessary tools to turn your canvas into a masterpiece. If your canvas is not plain, but just not as you'd like it to be, than you can use your tools to embellish it just a little more. Let your imagination run wild. You'll be given an opportunity to do a self-portrait, idealize your living space, re-create your work space, and define what you want in your relationships.

DAY 2

Today you get to paint your self-portrait. How do you see yourself? How do you want to see yourself? What colors, fabrics, words, pictures, images, feelings, and behaviors would you select to be you if you had the choice? Would you choose happy, sad, honest, empowered, energetic, fearful, courageous, productive, wealthy, healthy? Record your thoughts in your journal. If you'd like, try drawing or painting a picture of your life.

DAY 3

Today you get to create your living space. Will it be cluttered, neat, warm, receptive, light, bright, dark, or inviting? Forget about how it looks today. You get to start anew with the picture you want. Just for today, you get to call the shots. Your job is to do whatever you must to create the living space you want.

DAY 4

Today you get to create your work space. Will it be cluttered, organized, neat, homey, formal, or filled with photos and stuffed animals? Will there be flowers? Will they be real? Just for today, you get to call the shots. Your job is to do whatever you must to create the work space you want.

DAY 5

Today you get to create the relationships you want. What do you want in a relationship? Does it includes an intimate partner, spouse, close friends, children, parents? Look at your primary relationship and ask yourself, "What works? What doesn't?" What would you need to do to make it work? Are you willing to do what it takes to have the relationship you want? If necessary, are you willing to leave the union? Sometimes we overstay in our relationships because of fear. While I'm not encouraging you to leave, I am inviting you to explore whether you've stayed too long and what it would take to move on.

DAY 6

Today is your last chance this week to decorate your life. Be mindful of all that would enhance the already beautiful canvas, such as more flowers, pictures, little animals, treasured friends, social appointments, and greater connectedness to family.

DAY 7

Finally, here we are at day 7. Once again you're invited to rest, recharge, regroup, and review your week. What observations can you make about your canvas this week? Was the idea of being the artist in your life challenging? What worked for you? What didn't? Was there a day that seemed exceptionally hard? Why?

WEEK 29

Move Your Body

Thought for the Week
It's an esteemable act to move your body.

Affirmations for the Week
I love moving my body.
This week, I will move my body into healthiness.

Esteemable Actions for the Week

DAY 1

My heaviest weight ever was 145 pounds, and I was only twenty-six years old. I went from a size four to a size fourteen almost overnight. For some, 145 is not a lot of weight, but for my small frame, it was a lot of bulk to carry. And I got that way by design. It wasn't a conscious plan, but when you couple no exercise with more than enough food, you get a heavy body. I can't go back and change the past, but I can control my present. This week, the focus is on moving your body.

By no means is incorporating a daily practice of movement easy to implement. And there have been more than a few times when I've allowed myself to slip back into the "no movement consciousness." But more often than not, I know my body is a temple and I treat it that way. It's hard to say I love myself when I don't take care of my body.

Today I understand the value of being physically active, particularly when I don't want to be. It's critical to a healthy mind, body, and spirit. Regular movement keeps us in good shape, aids our digestion, assists our body in the regulatory process, reduces depression, increases energy, and makes us feel and look better.

For all the benefits, however, many of us don't exercise. Why not? Here are a few reasons. We think it'll take up too much time, cost too much, be too complicated, require too much effort, require too much energy. We don't have a gym and we can't afford a gym, or we don't have the proper clothes to wear to the gym. We think we're too fat, we're too skinny, we need support, we can't afford support, we don't know where to start, we don't want to do it alone, there are too many people at the gym, there are not enough people at the gym, it's co-ed, it's not co-ed . . .

So how do we get past the obstacles to moving our body? Here are some suggestions:

1. Create an intention to move daily. It all begins with a thought, a desire to take action. Visualize yourself walking, dancing, running, jumping, taking the stairs.

2. Plan and schedule your activities in advance. Consider planning your exercise schedule on Sunday for the entire week. You can always change it as the week progresses, but have a plan in place. For example, on Monday, walk briskly for thirty minutes; on Tuesday, do twenty-five jumping jacks; on Wednesday, dance to fast music for thirty minutes; and on Thursday, swim or hike. Then, every day, take the stairs instead of the elevator whenever possible.

3. Alternate activities in order to keep you motivated and so the process remains interesting and possibly fun. Not everything has to be fun. Sometimes your job is to do the right thing for yourself simply because it's the right thing. There will be days when it will

feel like a chore to move your body. Do it anyway. That's the esteemable act. It's easy to do what's easy; it's harder to do what's not. But what's not is sometimes what's best for you.

4. Small actions every day are the key. Baby steps lead to success over the long haul. Fifteen minutes of a fast walk, jumping around in place, or taking the stairs is better than nothing.

5. Celebrate every action you take. Always applaud yourself for taking any action, regardless of how small. We all respond to appreciation and it makes you want to keep trying.

6. Invite a friend to join you. Exercise sometimes goes better with friends. It helps you stay accountable and committed.

7. Watch television or listen to music. Sometimes I don't want to go to the gym, so I bring my FitBall and my weights in front of the television and work out.

8. Honor your agreement to yourself. There are always valid excuses for not going to the gym, running five miles, or playing volleyball, but there is no excuse for not moving your body. You simply have too many options.

This week, you're invited to create a plan for moving your body. That is your focus for this week. My hope is that, by the end of the week, you'll have an idea of what works for you in terms of exercise, what time is your best time for exercising, and how long your body can withstand the pressure. Daily, you'll progressively increase your movement, until on the sixth day you are doing more than you thought you could do.

DAY 2

Get started! Today is the first day of your daily practice of moving your body. Create your intention and do it on paper. For example, "Today I move my body toward good health—one day at a time." Schedule your activities for the rest of this week. For example, take a brisk walk or slow jog, climb stairs ten times a day, do jumping jacks, dance to music for thirty minutes, or lift weights while you're watching television. Create a movement log where you keep track of everything you do this week, from taking the stairs instead of the elevator to jogging on a track to lifting weights in the gym.

DAY 3

Alternate activities. If you did jumping jacks yesterday, walk fast for fifteen minutes today. Variety keeps you moving.

DAY 4

List three things you'll do today that get your body moving.

DAY 5

Today let's ramp it up. Do thirty minutes of some form of exercise. Afterward drink two glasses of water.

DAY 6

Invite a friend to come out to "play" with you: make an appointment to meet at the gym, or instead of meeting for lunch, go for a walk or a workout.

DAY 7

Here we are at day 7, and once again you're invited to rest, recharge, regroup, and review your week. What observations can you make about your willingness to move your body? Was it a hard week? What worked? What didn't?

Let Go of Addiction

Thought for the Week

Letting go of addiction is an esteemable act.

Affirmations for the Week

I deserve to be habit free.

This week, I will let go of any addiction
that stands in my way.

Esteemable Actions for the Week

DAY 1

Addiction, regardless of how we define it, robs us of the ability to make right choices. Whether we're addicted to drugs, alcohol, food, gambling, sex, love, other people's opinions, or old ideas, our lives are no longer our own. Because we're addicted, we do things we'd never normally do. The addiction decides where we go, when we'll go, whom we'll go with, how long we'll stay, and what we'll do once we are there.

For years I hated the word *addiction,* because I felt it connoted an immorality that didn't apply to me, a level of depravity that seemed like an overstatement. In time I let go of my dislike of the label and realized that regardless of what I called it—a habit, a dependency, or a craving—it still had the power to control my life in a way that was unhealthy and unacceptable. And I never realized how controlled I was by my addiction until I let go of it.

I recently spoke with a woman who hasn't had a drink in seventeen years or a cigarette in ten years, yet she is 150 pounds *over* her healthy weight. A man I coach has never had a drinking problem, but he smokes incessantly. Darian, a longtime friend of mine, is so controlled by what people think of her that she has had more plastic surgeries than most people I know—all in an effort to achieve what she perceives as the perfect look. Liv had surgery for a broken leg six months ago, and at the direction of her physician, she took pain pills several times a day. After months of taking them as prescribed, she started taking a few extras—every hour. When her doctor refused to give her another prescription, she found another source. She's now addicted to pain pills.

We live in a society that encourages excess, stress, fitting in, and being liked at any cost. It eventually backfires. When we bring together an unhappy person with a means of escape, we may get a habit.

Getting hooked is easy. Getting off is hard, but it can be done. Here are some suggested steps you can take if you are serious and ready to let go of your addictions:

1. Admit you have a problem. Before recovery can occur, there must be an admission that a problem exists.
2. Get help. Today help is available for all kinds of problems.
3. Listen to the people who have recovered from illnesses similar to yours.
4. Walk through the daily fears you'll encounter.
5. Be willing to stretch beyond your comfort zone. If you're not willing to do the footwork, it's not likely you'll succeed.
6. Talk about what's bothering you. You are as sick as your secrets.

We may not be the addict in our lives, but we've become controlled by someone else's addiction. The outcome is the same. We make choices based on that person's problem, particularly if it's a family member. We make excuses for this person's behavior and, without knowing it, support him or her in staying addicted and not taking responsibility for his or her actions. If this is you, get help.

This week, you're invited to examine any addictions or habits that might be controlling your life.

DAY 2

Before there can be recovery, there must be an admission that a problem exists. Is an addiction running your life? Or is there someone close to you with an addiction that affects you? Maybe it's an addiction to drugs, alcohol, gambling, prescription medication, sex, shopping, plastic surgery, or old ideas. Whatever it may be, have the courage to acknowledge its presence in your life.

DAY 3

Where can you go for help? Depending on your addictive condition, your first step might be your therapist, a therapeutic community, a rehabilitative facility, or a Twelve Step program. Today there is help for those with any problem imaginable, including those affected by someone else's addiction. Today your task is to pick up the phone and make a call or go to the Internet and get contact information. If you're in school, go to your guidance counselor. If you work for a company, contact its employment assistance program (EAP). If you have nowhere to go or are afraid to use the resources you have, contact a clergy member or a trusted neighbor. The key is to start somewhere and ask for help.

DAY 4

Wherever you go for help, be open to listening to the suggestions given, particularly from those who have walked the path before you.

DAY 5

Today is your day for collecting useful information regarding staying away from your addiction. When I was newly sober, I heard slogans like "One day at a time," "First things first," "Easy does it," and "Don't pick up the first drink." List three things you learned this week from the people you turned to for help.

DAY 6

Talk about what's bothering you. Whether you've sought help through an individual or a group, today is your day to tell the truth about your decision and your feelings about your life. Perhaps you've already started opening up. If so, keep up the good work and open up a little more. If you've not shared your situation with anyone yet, today is your day. Grab your journal and make notes about your feelings.

DAY 7

Here we are at day 7, and once again you're invited to rest, recharge, regroup, and review your week. What observations can you make about this week? Was the discussion of addiction uncomfortable? Was the thought of letting go too hard? What worked for you this week? What didn't? What day seemed extra hard? Why?

There Are No Mistakes in God's Universe

Thought for the Week

It's an esteemable act to know that everything
happens for a reason.

Affirmations for the Week

I know that everything happens for a reason.

This week, I will trust in the process.

Esteemable Actions for the Week

DAY 1

Sometimes when we're disappointed because we didn't get an outcome we wanted, it's hard to understand why it happened. It seems unfair that we try so hard to achieve our goals with little visible success. It's especially hard if we did our very best. "Why me?" we ask. "Why is this happening to me? What did I do wrong?"

There have been many times when I failed, made a mistake, or was rejected and inherently knew I must try again. I knew at my core that it wasn't time to give up without a fight even when I continually received rejection letters from literary agents, when it seemed like I'd never make it to the finish line during my first marathon race, and when my year-old marriage seemed likely to end in divorce court.

Nothing, absolutely nothing, happens in this world by accident, even if in the moment we can't make sense of the experience. There are often two levels of reasoning. There is a logical, secular explanation, such as we weren't prepared in the way we needed to be or we could have made some different choices. But there is also a spiritual, metaphysical accounting that suggests that whatever happens was for our highest and best good, regardless of outward appearances to the contrary. The spiritual reasons could be we weren't emotionally ready to go to the next level, we had more inner work to do, there were more important things to attend to before our dream could be realized, it wasn't the right time, or had we realized our dream, we would have missed another opportunity that we needed to experience.

Failing the California Bar exam repeatedly was one of the single most painful experiences of my life. But it provided me with my greatest opportunity. Had I passed that Bar exam, I'd be practicing law in California today, even though that's not what I really wanted to do. However, when I finally let go of the exam that appeared to be my reason for living, I awakened to a new and better life, a life I would have missed out on if I were sitting in a law office. Out of the darkness came the opportunity of a lifetime, which led me to coaching, speaking, training, consulting, and now, writing my second book. Self-esteem comes from doing esteemable acts, and it's an esteemable act to know that everything happens for a reason.

Perhaps at a later date I'll retake the California Bar exam, and perhaps not. How do you know whether to let a dream go or keep at it? And if you let go, how do you know when it's time to try again? There is no one-size-fits-all answer. There are many factors to be considered, including timing. If you're at this crossroads, take into account the following:

- Are you consumed with making your dream happen? During my struggle with the California Bar exam, my days and nights were consumed with preparing for the test, taking the test, waiting for the results of the test, then brooding because I failed it. I had no life and had become spiritually sick.

- How long have you worked to make it happen? How many attempts have you made? It's easy to give up after one or two tries. But sometimes the real lesson is in staying the course until you really know it's time to let go. I stopped counting after six attempts to pass the exam. Some people believed I should have stopped sooner; I know I was right on time. For me, stopping sooner would have been giving up, not letting go. I needed to know I had done everything I could in that moment.

- How does your obsession with making it happen affect your loved ones? Sometimes the price we pay is worth it—and sometimes it's not. Only you can decide. At the time I didn't have a family to consider; today I do. Maybe today my decision about pursuing the exam would be different—and maybe not.

- What are the financial implications? Health implications? Are you using your last dime, your family's savings, or your rent money? Are you borrowing lots of cash or have people stopped lending you money? Are you overly stressed to the point of exhaustion? Are you getting sick? These are questions to consider.

- Is it really your dream to make this happen? If so, sometimes it's worth everything to keep the dream alive. My dream was to become a lawyer licensed to practice in the state of New York. That happened in 1991. The California Bar exam was an afterthought in 1993.

- Does your life or livelihood depend on the success of this experience? At the time I thought so, because I had no other skills. The experience forced me to be creative and think about what I really wanted to do with my life.

- How do you know when you're ready to resume the process? The answer varies. However, the amount of time since your last attempt, whether you've been able to acknowledge your mistakes, whether you've been able to identify lessons learned, and whether you've been able to reach out for help are all factors to be weighed.

This week, you're invited to review an experience in light of the above.

DAY 2

Bring to mind a time you were disappointed because you didn't get an outcome you hoped for. How much effort did you put into your attempt? Perhaps you submitted five résumés with no luck. Maybe you applied to ten colleges and not one accepted you. Or maybe, like me, you sent sixteen query letters to literary agents and in return received sixteen form rejection letters. Write about the experience today.

DAY 3

Focusing on the situation mentioned in day 2, what's been the impact on your family, your friendships, your finances, and your health? Allow yourself to really think this through today, then write about it.

DAY 4

What makes you know this is a dream worth fighting for? Make a list of the pros and cons. What do you have to lose? What will you gain if you continue to move ahead? Is it worth the price?

DAY 5

List some reasons why you think you are going through this experience. Any lessons learned?

DAY 6

Today allow yourself to think through what would happen if you put your dream on hold temporarily. You may not think that you have the time or that you've already invested too much money to stop now. But perhaps if you continue as you are, more money and time will go to waste. Sometimes allowing time to come between you and the experience gives you a chance to regroup, reassess your strategy, and become spiritually and emotionally strong again.

DAY 7

Here we are at day 7, and once again you're invited to rest, recharge, regroup, and review your week. What observations can you make about the situation you're in? Was the idea of possibly letting go temporarily difficult for you to swallow? How did you feel when you looked at how your dream has and continues to affect others? What worked for you this week? What didn't? What day seemed extra hard? Why?

Walk Through Your Fear

Thought for the Week

Self-esteem comes from having the courage
to walk through your fear.

Affirmations for the Week

Fear no longer controls my life.

This week, I will have the courage to walk
through my fear.

Esteemable Actions for the Week

DAY 1

I've always been fearless, or so I thought. And as long as I had a
drink or a drug in my hand, that was true. Chemicals gave me the
courage to do the impossible, such as talk to people, feel my feelings, ask for what I needed, take what I wanted, be friendly and so-
ciable, speak up in a group, or simply function in the big scary
world. When my chemical support was removed, my courage disap-
peared. I felt helpless, unprotected, and unable to cope. It's amazing
how easy it is to be strong when you've got drugs in your system. At
other times, it was the power of a group that made me able to do the
seemingly impossible. Sadly, I also did bad things in groups that I
would never have done alone. I had the courage to hurt people, to

169

say mean things, to behave in a way that was inappropriate—all because the group was behind me.

Courage is a powerful state of being, and when used for good, it is an empowering consciousness to behold. I used to think courage was an absence of fear: I held my chest out pompously and claimed to be afraid of nothing. Today I know courage is a willingness to admit I'm afraid and then take the action to get through the fear, without the aid of chemicals and without purposefully hurting anyone along the way.

Fear can be beneficial. It can alert us to the dangers that lie ahead. Fear cautions us not to walk down a dark, desolate street alone or not to put our finger in a flame. It also keeps us paying our bills on time rather than running the risk of having no home, phone, or utilities. It keeps most of us willing to protect our children and pets in the same way we'd protect ourselves.

Fear can also stand in the way of our happiness, of our success, of our ability to love another person, of our ability to communicate effectively, and of our ability to really practice self-care. It keeps us stuck: we focus on why we can't do something rather than identifying ways to make it happen. Further, the consequences of fear are that our lives are not our own.

Why is fear so powerful? Because we deny its existence. We pretend we're not afraid, even when we are. It's the only emotion that convinces us that we don't have the emotion. So the more we deny it, the more powerful it becomes.

Fear shows up in many ways. In *Alcoholics Anonymous,* the Big Book, we read that fear reveals itself in one hundred different self-centered forms. So how do we recognize it? Here's a short list of phrases we use as substitutions for the word *fear*:

- I'm nervous.
- I'm embarrassed.
- I can't do it.

- It's too hard.
- I really didn't want to do it anyway.
- I'm apprehensive.
- I'm feeling trepidation.
- I was told I didn't have to do it.
- It's not my responsibility.
- I don't have to do anything I don't want to do.

Regardless of what we call it, fear, by any other name, is still fear. So how do we walk through fear?

- Acknowledge the fear.
- Break the task into small pieces. The easiest way to get through a fearful situation is to break it into smaller, more manageable, and less daunting pieces.
- Feel the fear and do something anyway. Fear is a very real human emotion, and it often surfaces when you're trying something new and different.
- Use your faith. If you don't have faith, use mine or find a friend who will encourage you to take action. Many people say they believe in God, yet they live a life tortured by fear. Why not use God to help you walk through your fear? That's how my faith has actually become stronger, by using God during those challenging times.

This week, you're invited to walk through something you're afraid to do.

DAY 2

Today acknowledge how often fear shows up for you. Be conscious of how many times you say, "I'm nervous," "I'm scared," "I can't do it," "I didn't want to do it anyway," "I'm embarrassed." Maybe you feel that way without voicing the words. Use your faith to help you get honest.

DAY 3

Make a list of tasks you're afraid to do: perhaps speaking up in a meeting, giving a presentation, going for the dream of your life, being open to meeting new people, saying no to someone, or saying yes to someone. Now break the task into little pieces. For example, let's say you're afraid of public speaking and you've been asked to give a presentation. Here are some suggested small steps:

1. Talk to the event planner to determine the purpose of the meeting, what's expected of you, who you'll be talking to, how long you'll be talking, whether there will be breaks, and anything else important for you to know to be fully prepared.
2. On paper, outline your talk. Determine how you'll open, how you'll close, and what points you'll cover.
3. Ask yourself whether you will include audience interaction, and if so, what kind.
4. Decide what visuals you will use, if any.
5. Practice, practice, practice!

When I ran marathons, it was scary. The very thought of walking, let alone running, 26.2 miles was daunting. So I broke the race into smaller, manageable pieces, and it became doable. I ran a half mile at a time, then a mile, then another mile, then another. Before I knew it, I had completed the 26.2-mile race, one baby step at a time. Think of a task you've been putting off because you are afraid you might fail, afraid you might succeed, afraid you won't do it perfectly, afraid someone will judge your effort, afraid to get started, or afraid of any other outcome. Use your faith to help you identify the small steps.

DAY 4

Today is your Feel the Fear and Do It Anyway Day. Select one thing on your list from day 3 and just do it. Use your faith to help you take an action.

DAY 5

Today you'll select another item from the list on day 3 and just do it. If you're adventurous, you might even consider doing one more little action. Use your faith to help you not give up.

DAY 6

Today list the advantages of walking through your fear regarding a task from day 4 or day 5. What could you gain from the experience? What could you lose if you don't even try?

DAY 7

Here we are at day 7, and once again you're invited to rest, recharge, regroup, and review your week. What observations can you make about your willingness to walk through your fear? What worked for you this week? What didn't? What day seemed extra hard? Why?

Make Peace with Your Parents

Thought for the Week

It's an esteemable act to make peace
with your parents.

Affirmations for the Week

I am grateful for my mother.

This week, I have the courage to make peace
with my family.

Esteemable Actions for the Week

DAY 1

I didn't always love her even though she is my mother. She wasn't there when I needed her, and when she was, we never seemed to connect. As a kid, when I was told I looked like my mother, I'd cringe with pain at the thought that we were actually cut from the same cloth. At eighteen I ran away from home. I would have left sooner, but when I was a minor, she could bring me home. And I didn't want that. So I grudgingly waited until that magical birthday—and I left. The only time we talked during the next ten years was when I needed something. It's a sad admission, but it's true.

For the first two years of my recovery, I was grateful for the women who had the courage to talk about how they didn't like their mothers and how their mothers had, in some way, impeded their growth and success. Being in their presence made me feel less alone, more like other women. That need to connect with people who hated as deeply as I did worked—until it didn't.

Over time, as I did the inner footwork required of healthy recovering people, my perspective changed. Luckily for me, I started listening to people who practiced the principles they learned in all their affairs, particularly with family. They showed me, by example, that I had a choice: I could continue to blame my mother for the life I had, which I hated, or I could clean up the debris and move on, taking some responsibility along the way.

Some of you will say, "But you don't understand. My situation is different." Your mother may have abused you or let your father abuse you. Maybe she was a drunk or a junkie, was never home, showered you with money but never love, was too controlling, made your father go away, or had any number of other problems. And please know I'm not denying that you are right, whether you're talking about your mother or your father. But making peace with your parents is not so much about them feeling good as it is about helping you live comfortably in your own skin. For many of us, regardless of how much we deny it, we become incapable of having a genuinely open, honest, respectful, and intimate relationship with anyone, man or woman, until we get clean with our parental relationships. How true a statement I have found that to be!

Many women have kids long before they are ready or just because they think they should. They are ill equipped to be mommies. And sometimes in the learning process, they make horrific mistakes, some irreparable. But one thing I learned for myself is this: we all have lessons to learn. My mother was not perfect. She made lots of mistakes. But today I know she did the best she could with what she had. And once I really got that, I became the beneficiary of so much goodness, abundance, and love. Indeed, I had to walk through the pain of my feelings and my history, but then I had a responsibility to truly let go.

Here are some suggestions, based on my own experience making peace with my mother and other family members:

1. Believe they did the best they could with the skills they had. My mother learned from her mother, who learned from her mother, who learned from hers. I can't imagine any woman is totally and completely equipped for motherhood. They do what they can with what they have. Ask yourself, "Could I have done better? Am I doing better?" Maybe and maybe not.

2. See them as human—imperfect, just like you and me. We all make mistakes. And we all want to be forgiven for our mistakes. When I stopped being so hard on myself, I was able to be less hard on my mother. What about you?

3. Know we have the tools to get through anything. The tools are available to work through relationships. All we need to do is ask for help.

4. Identify the payoff to holding on to the anger. Why do you want to hold on to the anger? Understanding the answer to that question will unlock the secret for you.

5. Identify the benefits to making peace. What's the payoff to resolving those hard-fought-for resentments?

6. Bring to mind something good in your family members, or something they did for you. My mother did so many good things for me, and when I became willing to appreciate them, I started to focus less on what she didn't do and more on what she did do.

You may be thinking, "What do I do if my parents have died? How do I make peace when they are no longer here?" In truth, there is no simple answer, because when they are gone, they are gone. I urge you to do the work while they are alive. If that's impossible because they've died, consider writing a letter. Think carefully about what you write, being particularly mindful to say what's in your heart. Don't let fear stop you from saying what you mean. After you've written the letter, sit with your feelings for a while, then ask to be released from the bondage of old wounds. This process may need to be repeated several times, and you may need to force yourself to be still and feel the feelings. It's worth the effort.

This week, you're invited to make peace with someone who needs your prayers.

DAY 2

Who are you estranged from in your family? Perhaps you haven't spoken to your mother, your father, or your sibling for years. Think about the last conversation you had with them. What happened to push you away? Was there some part you played in what happened? How were you hurt by them or their behavior?

DAY 3

Today explore what you get from not connecting with your family. What are the payoffs for being out of relationship with them? Make a list. What are some reasons for healing the relationship?

DAY 4

Is there anything that would make you willing to initiate the healing process? Why or why not? Write about it.

DAY 5

Write a letter to a family member expressing your feelings. Write about what hurt you, how they betrayed your trust, how they didn't care for you as they should have, and so on. Don't worry—you won't be sending it and no one but you will see it, so write exactly how you feel.

DAY 6

Today grab your journal and write a list of the payoffs for making peace with a family member. Share that list with a trusted friend.

DAY 7

Here we are at day 7, and once again you're invited to rest, recharge, regroup, and review your week. What observations can you make about your willingness to make peace with your parents? Was there anything you appreciated about this week? Anything that made you especially upset or angry?

Week 34

Walk Like You Talk

Thought for the Week

It's an esteemable act to walk like you talk.

Affirmations for the Week

My behavior is consistent with my words.

This week, I will do what I say I will do.

Esteemable Actions for the Week

DAY 1

The renowned author James Baldwin once said, "Children have never been good at listening to their elders, but they've never failed to imitate them." And, I add, ditto for adults.

It's easy to think that no one's watching us. It's safe and comfortable to think that what we do doesn't affect others. In fact, what we do does affect others, whether it's our kids, our partners, our pets, our friends, or our co-workers. I've often heard people say jokingly, "If you really knew how little people paid attention to you, you'd be disappointed." That sounds good in theory, but in reality, we are always an example of how to live in the world, whether we like it or not.

The first time I really understood that was when I returned home from a short business trip a few years ago. There was a lovely message on my voice mail from someone who had heard me speak at an event several weeks earlier. Her message was simply, "You're amazing. I caught a glimpse of you in the Dallas/Fort Worth airport when you were having trouble with the gate agent. Sorry I didn't get to say hello, but I noticed how well you handled what could have resulted in a really bad outcome. The next thing I knew, you and the agent were smiling and chatting. Bravo for walking like you talk."

The idea that I had been observed without knowing it was a little unsettling. Then my mind quickly switched to gratitude: I'd been caught doing what was perceived as the right thing—maybe once, twice, ten times, a hundred times? But more important, it made me question how often I'd been caught having a tantrum in public when I didn't get my way. How many times had I been overheard being rude to people who were only doing their jobs? It's food for thought.

It also got me thinking about how I behave at home. It's sometimes easy to do the right thing in public; it's quite another to practice what we preach behind closed doors.

Why is it important that we walk the way we talk?

1. When you walk like you talk, you feel better about you. Regardless of how many times you tell yourself you're a good person, a loving spouse, or someone deserving of respect, if you don't act deserving of respect, you won't feel deserving.

2. Your children pay more attention to what you do than what you say. Like it or not, your example is still the primary one they learn from.

3. There are many experts telling us how to behave, yet sometimes their example is less than exemplary. They seem to be saying, "Take my advice, but I'm not using it!" You become more credible if you behave in the way you tell others to behave.

4. It makes you someone *you* can respect.

There are also consequences to not walking like you talk. At some time in your life, I'm sure someone said to you, "Do as I say, not as I do." Perhaps it was a parent, a teacher, a rabbi or member of the clergy, a coach, your big brother or sister, or just someone you looked up to. You listened to them because you trusted them and you believed that if they said to do something, it was the right thing. Then, maybe at a later date, you discovered they weren't doing what they told you to do. You felt betrayed and lied to. Remember the first time your mother, father, sister, or brother told you not to drink, and then you saw him or her with a glass in hand? Or remember when you were told smoking was bad, yet everyone around you was smoking? Or remember when someone first told you that all people are created equal, but then you witnessed prejudice? There are consequences to not walking like you talk.

Adults learn from one another and kids learn from adults. I'm often asked when speaking to parents of teenagers, "How can we help our kids feel better about themselves? How can we build self-esteem in our children?" Contrary to popular belief, we can't build a kid's self-esteem. Self-esteem can't be taught. However, we can create a space for kids to grow into their best selves. We can teach them to be decent human beings who care about others, talk to them, listen to them, and walk like we talk.

There are some who will quickly stand up and say, "I don't care what people think when they see me." They say, "There is way too much emphasis on what others think" and "It's not my responsibility to be a role model for the world's kids." That's true, within reason. However, like it or not, we are examples. We each play a part in co-creating the world we live in.

This week, let's examine ways to walk more like you talk.

DAY 2

Examine your behavior today. What message are you communicating? If people were to catch you in public without you knowing it, what would they be a witness to? How would you behave in traffic when someone cuts you off? How would you behave when you're not getting your way while dealing with a vendor? If people were to listen in on one of your phone calls, what would they hear? How would you be speaking to the person on the other side? If they saw you in a restaurant when the server delivered the wrong entrée, what would they catch you doing?

DAY 3

Think of someone who walks differently than they talk. Perhaps you were at a conference and the speaker from the platform portrayed one image, and then once off the stage, had a different persona. Or maybe you personally know a public figure who is one way at home and another on television. Or maybe you know someone who speaks of family values and has a mistress on the side. What are your thoughts about that person?

DAY 4

Now think of someone who walks like they talk. Perhaps the speaker's principles are the same on or off the platform, or the celebrity or public figure is the same at home as on the television. Or maybe that neighbor who talks of family values is really respectful of his or her family in every way. What are your thoughts about that person when you discover their behavior is congruent with their words?

DAY 5

What can you do today to bring your actions more into alignment with your words? List three things. Now do one of them today.

DAY 6

Whose behavior are you imitating? What aspects of another person have you copied? Consider the positive as well as the negative traits. Maybe you have a short temper and your mentor was someone who, when things didn't go her way, screamed at her subordinates. Are you that way because you saw someone walk that way? Perhaps it's the way you carry yourself. Was there someone who had a style you liked that you copied? Did they dress professionally, provocatively, or casually? Do you?

Today stop and think about who's imitating you. Who are you influencing in the way you dress, behave, and talk? If your kids are cursing, where have they learned it? If they are drinking and using drugs, who's their primary role model? If your son is violent, who is teaching him such things? If your daughter is in an abusive relationship, how did she learn to hate herself so much? Who were her role models? While you may not have taught them intentionally, I invite you to think about how you walk around your kids.

DAY 7

Today is your Four Rs Day, time once again for you to rest, recharge, regroup, and review your week. What observations can you make about your behavior this week? Did you walk like you talk? If not, what stopped you from doing so? What day seemed extra hard? Why?

WEEK 35

Mirror, Mirror, on the Wall

Thought for the Week

It's an esteemable act to see yourself clearly.

Affirmations for the Week

I am not afraid to know who I really am.

This week, I am willing to see the part I play
in my interactions with others.

Esteemable Actions for the Week

DAY 1

My friend was upset because her brother called her controlling. "Who does he think he is?" she said. "He had no right to say that about me."

"Is it true? Are you controlling?" I asked.

"I don't think I am," she said. "I'm just passionate about things."

"Why did he call you controlling? What did he say you did?"

"I told him I didn't like how he was raising his daughter."

"Is it possible he could have perceived your words as controlling?" I asked.

"I doubt it, but if he did, it was his fault for interpreting my words that way."

This could have been a scenario with you and a friend, you and a family member, or you and a co-worker. It's any scenario where you are seen one way but you perceive yourself differently. Do you know who you are? Do you know how your behavior affects others? We go through life seeing ourselves as we want to be seen, not always as we are. Frequently that means seeing ourselves as the good guy, the one wronged, the one taking the high road, the person who is misunderstood. Yet there are times when our attitude, our tone of voice, our body language, and the words we use turn us into the wrongdoer.

Having the courage to continuously examine our behavior, our motives, and even our thoughts is an esteemable act. And it's difficult because we're asked to see past our filters and defenses to the truth of who we are in the moment. Our filters protect us. By their very nature, they distort our vision. We tend to see only the good. It's important to acknowledge our assets, but unless we can balance our perception, we aren't able to see our part in problems that occur. We then become challenged to understand why people respond to us the way they do. For example, I had a bad habit of interrupting people when they were talking. I'd walk up and jump into an existing conversation without concern for people's feelings. To me, that wasn't rude or inconsiderate. It was just the way I was, and most of the time, I had no idea I was doing it. I was oblivious to my behavior and its impact on others until one day someone actually called my attention to what I did. It was a painful realization and one that made me more aware of my behavior.

Self-examination is life transforming, so why don't more of us do it? We mistakenly believe that if there is need for improvement, we're defective. So we walk around thinking we're perfect while acting imperfect and inflicting casualties along the way. The process of self-discovery happens over time. Here are three common phases:

- The *open phase* is where you assess who you are. While we never reach a place of perfection, at this level of discovery, you are the most willing to acknowledge your assets and liabilities. You see yourself as you are and you're willing to change when appropriate. Because you see yourself clearly, there are no secrets that prevent you from living a full and useful life.

- The *secret phase* is where you know of something that needs improvement, but others don't. In your heart of hearts, you believe if you keep it to yourself, no one will ever know. The problem is that secrets have a way of surfacing and affecting our lives, whether covertly or overtly. You are aware of the problems you have, even if you choose not to address them.

- The *denial phase* is where others know of your character flaws, but you don't or you choose to ignore them.

- The *unidentified phase* is where a problem exists under the surface and neither you nor anyone else really knows about it. It hasn't been identified yet.

The opportunity for growth comes when we are willing to see ourselves as we are and make changes when necessary. How can we see ourselves clearly? We begin by taking an honest inventory to catalog our strengths—traits that make us effective—and our challenges—traits that get in the way of our effectiveness. The inventory requires that we always be on the lookout for fear. Fear will convince us there's no need for self-improvement, that we're fine just the way we are. And while we may be wonderful, there is always room for personal improvement. Fear will also tell us to stop the process of self-discovery when it feels too real. Resist the temptation to do so. Keep going. Any pain we may feel is only temporary and will cease to control us as we work through the process.

The inventory process activates two powerful forces: humility and honesty. Humility, because we become teachable, open to learning about ourselves. Honesty, because we have the courage to see what's real. This week, you're invited to discover *you*.

DAY 2

List five of your strengths, things that you like about yourself. Remember, this list should come from you. You may get ideas from what others have told you in the past, but the list should only contain what you believe is true. For example, are you self-motivated, talkative, helpful, organized, friendly, creative, assertive, and considerate of others' feelings? Are you loyal, a hard worker, or a good listener? How do you see yourself?

DAY 3

List five of your challenges, things that if improved would make you even more effective than you already are. Be aware of the tendency to get down on yourself as you're going through this important phase of the process. It's just information that you can do something about if you're willing. For example, are you demanding, unorganized, argumentative, passive, or inconsiderate of others' feelings? Are you a gossip, lazy, or overly involved in others' problems? You may have noticed that some of the traits perceived as strengths can also be viewed as challenges. It's all in how you see it.

DAY 4

We often learn about our behavior by the way we act under pressure. Today be open to how you respond to stress. Perhaps you were disappointed by someone, made a big mistake, or caused a problem to occur. Be aware of how you handled the situation. Write about it.

DAY 5

What did you discover about yourself from yesterday's exercise? What could you have done differently? Use that newfound knowledge to approach today differently. How will you use what you learned?

DAY 6

We get information about ourselves when placed in certain positions. What kind of leader are you? What kind of subordinate are you? Do you take direction well? Do you give it well? How does the way you lead or follow affect your interactions with other people?

DAY 7

Today is your Four Rs Day, time once again to rest, recharge, regroup, and review your week. What attitudes, behaviors, beliefs, or assumptions surfaced this week? Was there a day more challenging than the others? What one thing did you learn about yourself?

WEEK 36

A Full and Thankful Heart

Thought for the Week

It's an esteemable act to have a full
and thankful heart.

Affirmations for the Week

I have a full and thankful heart.

This week, I will be open to opportunities
to be grateful.

Esteemable Actions for the Week

DAY 1

Hal Marley, one of my most treasured and beloved mentors, often spoke of gratitude. "You must develop an attitude of gratitude," he'd repeatedly say. "There is always something to be grateful for."

Once in early recovery, when I was complaining about a meeting I attended, he said, "There is no such thing as a bad meeting." A little perplexed by that statement, I continued to listen. "Because in each and every case," he said, "there is something to be learned. There is new wisdom, where you discover something for the first time. There is the confirmation of existing insights, when something you already know is reaffirmed. Then," he continued, "there is negative instruction, where you see examples of how you don't want to be." His perspective that everything is a gift is powerful. And despite his daily challenges, even on his deathbed in February 2002, Hal's attitude was one filled with gratitude.

Why the emphasis on gratitude? Because life is short and we never know when we will make our transition to the next life. To be sure, there is absolutely nothing wrong with spending our days, weeks, and months angry at someone for hurting us or being mad because something didn't go our way. But why waste our valuable energy? Anger takes up space; gratitude creates space. Unquestionably, life is unfair, and yes, there are things we want that we can't have. But when we shift the focus to what we have rather than what we don't, our consciousness is transformed. Ironically, we then open ourselves up to new ways of making happen what we want to happen.

There are more benefits to having a thankful heart:

- You become a magnet for goodness because you are looking for the good in your life and are open to finding it.
- Gratitude gives rise to more gratitude.
- You are more fun and interesting to be around because you're not always complaining about your rotten life.
- You feel empowered because you're taking positive action.
- When you are willing to help yourself, others want to help you.
- Gratitude lifts the spirit, opens the heart, and nourishes the soul. Also, when you're grateful, it's easier to feel good about yourself because you are willing and able to see the good in others.
- While being grateful doesn't mean you're not hurt or upset by life situations, it means you understand that life's difficulties are part of your experience. You feel the pain, and then get on with life.

With all these benefits, why do so many of us choose to focus on the glass being half empty? What gets in the way of gratitude?

- It's easy to focus on the negative.
- Feeling ungrateful is comfortable and familiar.

- Feeling ungrateful becomes a habit.
- You like the attention you get.
- You want an excuse to escape through drugs, alcohol, food, and so on.
- You don't know how to stop feeling ungrateful.
- You need help breaking the cycle and are afraid to ask.

How do we get to that place of having a full and thankful heart? Despite all that goes on in our day-to-day lives, how do we get to see the glass as half full rather than half empty? Here are some useful steps to consider:

1. Know that gratitude is an action—one to be practiced daily. For example, you don't write a gratitude list once and then forget about it. It helps when it becomes a daily or weekly practice. My mentor Peggy has me writing a weekly gratitude list. When she first made the suggestion, the arrogant part of me thought, "Why should I do that? I've been sober a long time, and I don't need that kind of direction. Plus, most of the time I'm grateful." One of the benefits of working with a mentor, a sponsor, or a coach who has walked the path before you is their insight. They see what you often can't—even with years of experience under your belt. It's easy to lose sight of your blessings when you get caught up in the day-to-day stuff of life. You simply forget. They remind you. A gratitude list is a small and gentle reminder of what is really important in life.

2. Be willing to see the good. It's easy to focus on the seemingly bad. It takes effort to see the good, whether it's the good in a person or a situation.

3. Say thank you every chance you get. Thank you goes a long way. First, it softens your heart because it forces you to appreciate something about someone else. Second, it makes others feel valued. They will often reciprocate, and even if they don't, your act of thoughtfulness goes a long way in nourishing your soul.

4. Make an effort to see something positive in every situation. That doesn't mean you must always be happy and walk around with a smile on your face. It means you make an effort to acknowledge what you have to be thankful for.

This week, work on cultivating an attitude of gratitude.

DAY 2

Write a gratitude list. Identify fifteen things you are grateful for today. Why not make this a weekly spiritual practice? Perhaps each Monday, list fifteen things you were grateful for during the preceding week.

DAY 3

As you go through this day, be aware of little things that you have to be grateful for. Perhaps you had help completing a project, you got something you wanted, or you were able to handle a difficult situation better than you had in the past. Identify seven little things you are grateful for today.

DAY 4

Think of one nice thing someone did for you today. What do you have in your life that makes you feel good? Is there a person who you love to be with, someone who makes you smile or laugh? Take a moment and make a list.

DAY 5

Some days it'll be easy to think of twenty things you're grateful for, and some days coming up with one item will be a challenge. Today may be one of those days. If so, simply write down that you're grateful for your ability to read this book. Some people can't read. Then chalk it up to one of those days. But if it's a gratitude-filled day, why not splurge and list fifty things you are grateful for throughout your life?

DAY 6

In your esteemable acts journal, describe something that happened within the last twenty-four hours that you're grateful for. If you can't think of anything, extend your net a little wider to include the last week, month, or year. Consider also looking beyond the obvious for things to be grateful for. The answer might be something you rarely think about, like being able to see, being able to walk, having a job, or not having a job so you have time to do what you want. For example, at this very moment, I'm grateful you're reading this book.

DAY 7

We're at the day for you to rest, recharge, regroup, and review your week. What observations can you make about your ability to be grateful this week? What day seemed extra hard? Why?

Be Here Now

It's an esteemable act to keep your mind
where your body is.

Affirmations for the Week

I give my attention to what I'm doing
in the moment.

This week, I will be fully present for my life.

Esteemable Actions for the Week

DAY 1

Have you ever been in a conversation with someone who wasn't
there? Have you ever been in a conversation with someone and you
weren't there? Have you ever been in a meeting and no one was
there? Most likely, you can unequivocally say yes to all of the above.
From time to time, and more often for some of us, we allow something outside of ourselves to distract us from what's important in
the moment. I often allow myself to become distracted. I allow
something to take me on a mental detour, whether I'm diverted by
other people's behavior or drawn into their drama. All these diver-
sions mean my mind is not where my body is.

When we allow ourselves to be distracted from what's happening in the moment, those around us suffer. People are affected, including our children, our spouses, our partners, our friends, our co-workers, or anyone we might be connecting with in the moment. When we go astray mentally or emotionally, we send a message to the person that he or she doesn't matter. That he or she is not important enough to hold our attention. Our words may say "you matter," but our actions scream something else.

Not long ago, I was sitting in a meeting when a honking began outside the window. It was loud and continuous. Many of the attendees, including me, became obsessed with the noise for the entire hour and a half. The honking was a condition we could not control, but we could control our reactions to it. We gave each other looks and whispered about the noise. We got so bothered by the outside condition that we ourselves ultimately became the distraction. Perhaps we were justified in being disturbed. But in truth, each of us had a choice as to whether to give away our power.

We each made a decision, conscious or otherwise, to allow a condition to control our experience. I allowed my attention to be stolen right out from under me. Those of us who chose to be distracted suffered because we missed out on the valuable information offered by the speaker and instead spent the entire time being angry about something we couldn't control. The presenter suffered because he was never able to recapture the attention of the fifteen or twenty people who went along with me for the mental ride. It was a lose-lose situation for all concerned.

Here are some other consequences of not being fully present:

- You miss opportunities to connect in ways that can only happen when you're actively listening.
- You miss useful information that could help you get through a rough period.

- You're misinformed, giving rise to misunderstandings because you only have part of the story.

What can we do to be more present? How can we bring our mind more in alignment with our body?

- For starters, admit your mind is not always where your body is. Denying any problem is a prescription for failure.
- Become aware of those times when your attention is diverted in another direction. Call it what it is!
- Be willing to see the damage to yourself, to your relationships, and to your serenity when you are not fully present. Get honest about how it affects you and others. A bold move is to ask someone you're in a relationship with how your behavior affects him or her.
- Be a careful and attentive listener. Listen to understand, not to judge.
- Practice quieting your busy mind. The noise in the brain is sometimes so overwhelming that we simply must shut it off.
- Practice staying in the moment. Hold your attention. When your mind wanders, gently bring it back.

This week, I invite you to practice being here now.

DAY 2

Bring to mind a time when your body wasn't where your mind was. What happened? What drew your attention away from where you were? What did you miss out on? What could you have done differently?

DAY 3

Today be aware of how often you are distracted. Perhaps during an important meeting you were thinking about what you're having for lunch. Maybe during lunch you're thinking about work. Maybe when you're with the kids, your attention was diverted to something else that made you not able to give them your full attention.

DAY 4

You don't live in a vacuum; your behavior often affects other people. Think back on your example from day 2. Who was affected by your behavior?

DAY 5

Practice quieting your mind. There are many benefits to having a quiet mind. List three or four, and today practice quieting your mind every time it gets busy.

DAY 6

Practice staying in the moment today. You may find it challenging at first, but after a while, it'll become easier. Whenever your mind wants to move away from where your body is, gently bring it back. What one tool for staying in the now will you practice today?

DAY 7

Today is your Four Rs Day, time once again for you to rest, recharge, regroup, and review your week. What observations can you make about your ability to be in the present moment? What worked? What didn't work? What day seemed extra hard? Why? For some of you, this day will seem just a little more challenging than those that came before. Nonetheless, I urge you to take this day to practice the four Rs.

WEEK 38

Breakthroughs

Thought for the Week

It's an esteemable act to have the courage
to break through to the other side.

Affirmations for the Week

I am breaking through right now.

This week, I will break through the barriers
that stand in the way of my own good.

Esteemable Actions for the Week

DAY 1

Last year I attended a weeklong spiritual conference at Asilomar, a beautiful retreat facility south of Monterey on the coast of California. For many years I heard about how fantastic an encounter Asilomar was, but attending always conflicted with other events. This year I created an intention to attend. And I did. What a magnificent experience it was.

Sometimes I just show up for a happening and walk away with whatever is my due. There is always something to be gained if my mind and heart are open—no matter what. But more often than not, I take control of my experience. I go into the situation seeking an answer to a question I have. It is on those occasions that I experience the most. I get what I need, and then some.

During the retreat, I had many chances to walk through my fear and be open to new and different ways of doing things. The most profound breakthroughs came in a combined physical and emotional form.

On the last day of the conference, we were told that we were going to break one-inch plywood boards with our hands. Immediately my mind slammed shut at the thought of breaking a board. "They can't make me do it," I thought. Yet while my mind said no, my body stayed put and listened to what the workshop facilitator had to say. Then he quickly shifted from the topic of breaking boards to the idea of breaking through any problem we face, such as walking through a feeling, being fully present during an experience, or seeking out a new opportunity. He also talked about breakthroughs in terms of things that block us from our own good. What I took away from his sharing was the following:

- Recognize the need for change. If there is no need for change, no breakthrough can occur.
- Be willing to break through. Yes, it's hard, and it's worth it.
- Stay focused on where you want to be, not on the obstacles that stand in your way. Keep the dream alive.
- Remain centered. When you're off balance—physically, emotionally, or mentally—it's hard to break through.
- Get support. While you probably can do it alone, the stronger the support, the more rewarding the breakthrough.

I thought about the times in my life when I broke through a barrier. Each time I knew I needed to make a change, finally accepted it, and was willing to do the work. I focused on the goal, I used God to center me, and I had the support of others. I got through school, I finally passed the Bar exam, I ran both marathons, I got published, I got sober, I lost weight—in every case this formula worked.

Reflecting back on that workshop, when it came time to break the board, surprisingly I was willing to try. I wasn't able to break the board the first time because I focused on the obstacles. We were told to write the obstacle on one side of the board, and that's where my attention was placed. I got locked into why I couldn't do whatever it was the board represented. I couldn't see past the problem to the solution. I was weaving nervously back and forth, unable to get centered.

On the second try, I broke through the plywood. It was a sweet success shared by my team, which was my support. What made this second attempt successful? I was centered, used my support system, and was focused not on the board, but past it to where I wanted to be.

What breakthroughs are you waiting to experience? This week, you're invited to break through to the next level.

DAY 2

Identify a problem that until now you've not been able to penetrate. What stands in your way? Write about it today.

DAY 3

Today is your day to focus on where you want to be. What would a breakthrough in this area look like? How will you know when you get there? How will you feel? Can you taste the feeling? What will happen for you when you break through?

DAY 4

Today practice getting centered. How does that look to you? What does *centered* mean to you? What tools can you use to help you get centered? How will you use these tools? Write out your answers.

DAY 5

What kind of support can you garner to help you in your breakthrough? Who specifically can you ask for help? What kind of help do you need from each person? Before you ask for help, be clear as to what you need from each person. When asking for help, always be mindful that other people are busy, so you need to go with a specific request and make sure you appreciate them for their time and assistance, regardless of how seemingly small the request. No one has to do anything for us, and it's a gift when they do.

DAY 6

Today is your Breakthrough Day. You're prepared with everything you need to break through to the next level in your life. Go do it. Let go of the stuff that stands in your way and start fresh. You can do it!

DAY 7

Once again, today you're invited to rest, recharge, regroup, and review your week. What observations can you make about your breakthrough week? Was it useful? Was one day more difficult than another? Why?

WEEK 39

Wisdom to Know the Difference

Thought for the Week
It's an esteemable act to pick your battles
carefully.

Affirmations for the Week
I accept what I can't change and change what I can.

This week, I will practice knowing when to take
action and when to let go and accept
what I can't change.

Esteemable Actions for the Week

DAY 1

We arrived as scheduled at the hotel of our choice for a two-week stay. It's always been one of our favorites. My husband and I checked into our room, only to discover we were located directly above the garbage dump, the loading dock, and the motorcycle pit. As I've learned to do, I took responsibility for my feelings and called the manager for assistance.

"We're regular visitors to this hotel," I said. "Can you move us to another room, please?"

"I'm sorry. I'm not able to change your room without assessing an additional $250 charge. That's the hotel's policy."

A little put off by his unwillingness to accommodate us, I asked, "Is it hotel policy to put regular customers over the garbage dump?"

Undisturbed by my obvious disapproval, he simply said, "There is nothing we can do for you at this time. You can check back with me in few days."

"What about a dinner voucher for my husband and me for the inconvenience? It's very noisy over the loading dock, and the smell from the garbage dump seeps into our window," I said.

"No, I'm sorry. We're not able to provide that for you at this time. I can, however, offer you a free drink at the pool."

When I got off the phone, I was livid and gave myself permission to be mad for about an hour. Then I read Step Three and recited the Serenity Prayer.

> Step Three: Made a decision to turn our will and our lives over to the care of God *as we understood Him.*

> Serenity Prayer: God, grant me the serenity to accept the things I cannot change, the courage to change the things I can, and the wisdom to know the difference.

In that moment, I thought, "What can't I change?" First, I couldn't change the hotel manager's mind. I asked, he said no. Second, I couldn't stop the noise from the garbage dump, the unloading of trucks, or the motorcycles revving up. And third, I couldn't get another room without paying more money.

Then I thought, "What can I change?" All I could think of was myself and my attitude. That was it. I repeated the Serenity Prayer and knew I had a choice—actually, lots of choices. What were my choices? To move to a different room and pay the extra fee. To stay in the room and accept the situation as is. To stay in the room, complain for two weeks, allow the resentment to destroy my vacation, and then blame the manager. Or demand my money back and go to another hotel. They were all valid choices. Some were better than others. And I could make the choice. The wisdom to know the difference is about having the courage to choose wisely and carefully. It's knowing what I can control and what I can't. After talking it over with my husband, we decided to pay the extra money and move to a more comfortable room.

There are times when it's appropriate to fight a battle because of principle. There are times when it's best to let go and claim victory in the letting go. Knowing when to do which is the challenge, and the gift. The wisdom to know the difference.

All we can change is ourselves: our attitude, our behavior, our feelings, and our beliefs. Nothing more. We can't change other people's attitudes, behaviors, feelings, or beliefs. This week, you're invited to practice knowing the difference.

DAY 2

In this twenty-four hours, be aware of how often you allow people or situations to control your experience—how frequently you get mad at someone and your entire day is ruined. Maybe it's the weather, an argument with a friend, or that someone cut you off in traffic. Make note of how many times today you refuse to accept something you couldn't change.

DAY 3

Today be aware of how often you allow people or situations to control your experience or make you mad and you don't take an action to change what you can. Maybe you could have told them they hurt you, asked them not to talk to you a certain way, or said that their behavior is unacceptable—but you didn't. Make note of how many times today you allowed fear of what someone would say stop you from changing a situation or speaking up for yourself.

DAY 4

Think of a situation in the past seven days where you allowed something or someone to ruin your experience. Perhaps it was a newspaper article, a television program, an election, or a movie. Why was that a battle you chose to fight? It's not to your advantage to fight every battle. There are times when you'll go to the mat, and there are other times when you won't. Learning to pick your battles wisely is an esteemable act.

DAY 5

One way to change an unhealthy behavior is to practice doing the opposite. In some cases, it will mean speaking up for yourself, and at other times, it will mean being silent and allowing your feelings to pass. Identify a situation where your choices are to accept something you can't change and to change something you can. What is within your power? What is within your control? How will you resolve the situation? If you are a Twelve Stepper, now's your chance to really work Step Three.

DAY 6

Today I invite you to practice taking dominion in your life. Begin with the situation in day 5. Yesterday you identified your choices, today go act on them.

DAY 7

Here we are at day 7, and once again you're invited to rest, recharge, regroup, and review your week. What observations can you make about your ability to know when to accept things you can't change and when to take an action? Was the idea of acceptance difficult? What about the idea that there is always something you can do? What worked for you this week? What didn't? What day seemed extra hard? Why?

WEEK 40

Learn from Your Mistakes

Thought for the Week

Self-esteem comes from learning
from your mistakes.

Affirmations for the Week

I know that everything is in divine order.

This week, I will learn from my mistakes.

Esteemable Actions for the Week

DAY 1

It was January 17, the day after my birthday. The morning started off well. I went to the gym at 5:00 a.m., checked e-mails before 7:30 a.m., and then sat down prepared to spend the next five hours writing. I was in a great mood and ready to go. Then my computer started to shut down—all by itself. Luckily I have another computer—a laptop—and the computer guy was scheduled to come over later in the day for a routine checkup. I logged on to my laptop, and then it happened . . . what anyone who relies on technology dreads . . . a virus. The virus completely corrupted my office computer—all my files, including client records, presentation documents, and manuscripts. It was a nightmare. And it got worse. I also needed a new computer.

There are days when all of our plans go smoothly; we feel in sync with life, and everything goes our way. Then there are days when it all falls apart and the best we can do is to ride it out, knowing this too shall pass. We make plans, and our plans take a detour in another direction. Life's setbacks are numerous, including dealing with a computer virus or other technology problems, the breakup of a relationship, an eviction notice, being late for an important appointment, or an unexpected bill. If you're having one of those days, here are some suggestions to help you get through to the other side:

1. Feel your feelings, every single one of them. When my computer virus hit, I didn't pretend it was no big thing nor did I pretend not to be hurt or angry. I cried for two solid hours, repeating constantly, "I can't believe this is happening to me." Having the courage to own your feelings in the moment helps you to get through to the other side a lot quicker.

2. Journal about your feelings. There's something magical about putting pen to paper. Write from your feeling place. Don't edit your words; no one will see this except you.

3. Pray. Ask for God's guidance. The idea here is to connect with that still, small voice within you, whatever you call it. There are no rules as to how you connect. What I've found to be useful is to find a quiet space. When there is a lot of noise around you, it's hard to tap into your intuitive voice, the one that steers you in the direction that's appropriate for you.

4. If prayer doesn't work for you, read something positive. This allows you to create a space within yourself so that a solution can enter. What usually works for me is reading Step Ten followed by Step Six in *Twelve Steps and Twelve Traditions,* or if the book is not close at hand, I generally listen to inspirational tapes.

5. Call a friend who will allow you to vent. Left to your own thoughts, you get more toxic. It's hard to solve the problem with the consciousness that helped to create the problem. The idea of having

someone shed light in the form of a solution or a suggestion can be helpful. Sharing in a nonjudgmental environment allows you to hear yourself, which ultimately helps you to get on with the business of living.

6. When all else fails, take a nap or watch a mindless television program purely for its entertainment value. Clear your mind long enough for sanity to return.

7. Have the courage to ask the tough questions. After my entire computer was destroyed because of a virus, I ranted about people who have nothing better to do than create viruses. I then needed to ask myself the following:

   - Could I have done something differently? Yes. All of my files should have been backed up. For me, paper backup is needed as well.

   - Were there red flags I didn't pay attention to or chose not to see? Yes. My computer had been acting strange for a while. At the very least, I should have backed everything up when I first noticed there was a problem.

   - Was there help available that I ignored? No. I had actually hired several computer consultants who never noticed a problem was brewing. I relied on the advice of experts.

   - Do I have personality traits that caused me to make the choices I made? Yes. I was in fear of spending more money on an elaborate data storage system. Plus, on some level, I thought it could never happen to me.

   - Could I have invested money in something that could have helped prevent this problem? Yes. I could have purchased a network data storage system or an online backup program.

8. Get into the solution. With a writing deadline and two client engagements scheduled within a week of the occurrence, I couldn't afford to pity myself for long. What could I do? I told my clients what happened and asked that they resend their documents. I recreated presentation materials as best I could. I checked my laptop

to see whether I had duplicate documents, and in some cases, I did. I ordered a new computer and saved everything on my laptop to floppy disks. I learned from my mistake.

This week, you have the opportunity to learn from your mistakes. Perhaps you haven't made any big mistakes yet. And you may not need these recovery tools just yet. If that's the case, you can fast-forward to the next week and return to this one when you need it, or you can read on and take what you can for that inevitably stormy day.

DAY 2

What went wrong today or this week? Write about it and allow yourself to feel whatever feelings come up.

DAY 3

Today is the day to create a spiritual opening, so you can eventually figure out what your next right action will be. Use whatever tools are at your disposal and appeal to you, such as talking to God, reading positive and inspirational material, listening to inspirational or motivational tapes, or calling a friend.

DAY 4

Ask the hard questions, starting with "What could I have done differently?" "Was there a part I played?" "Was there something I missed or intentionally chose not to see?"

DAY 5

What can you do to get into the solution? What actions can you take to minimize the damage done? What can you do to prevent this from happening again?

DAY 6

What lessons did you learn from the experience?

DAY 7

Today is your day to rest, recharge, regroup, and review your week. What observations can you make about your willingness to learn from your mistakes? What worked for you this week? What didn't? Was one day more challenging than another?

WEEK 41

Honesty: A Necessary Tool for the Journey

Thought for the Week

Self-esteem comes from having the courage
to live an honest life.

Affirmations for the Week

I am an honest person.

This week, I will live the value of honesty.

Esteemable Actions for the Week

DAY 1

Recently I was watching a popular television show in which the story line and the characters were all going through transition. Three political candidates were preparing for the first stop on the primary election tour. Only one would walk away with the party's nomination for president. All three were at odds about a certain issue, an issue that would negatively affect many people—but not the people they were speaking to on their first stop on the primary trail. Television viewers watched each candidate struggle to decide how to handle it. Only one had the courage to tell the truth to his constituents, knowing full well the consequences. The other two listened to their handlers and lied to the voters. The candidate who spoke the truth barely made a dent in the polls. He wasn't the

217

popular choice. The other two went on to compete against each other, and one of them won the election.

How often do you slant the truth in an effort to be liked? To get something you want? To get votes? To make a little extra money?

We all want to be liked. It feels good when people like us. We get invited to do things and go places, people don't gossip about us, and we're part of the "in" crowd. However, this need to be liked can compel us to comply with things we don't agree with—perhaps even things we don't believe in—and not speak up about something we know to be an injustice. When being liked or approved of is the driving force of our existence—for whatever reason—we sometimes do things that go against our values.

I first discovered the value of telling the truth and how much courage it takes about twenty-five years ago. The lesson for me was painful yet memorable. Perhaps because I was on the receiving end. My mentor Louise Robertson was the first person who had the courage to tell me the truth about my inappropriate behavior, the poor choices I made, and how I affected others. Her candor provided me with not only useful feedback that changed my life but also an example of how, if you really love someone, you have a responsibility to tell him or her the truth. And with truth comes risk of loss.

By having the courage to tell me the truth, she helped me step out of the darkness into the light. When I did something well, she told me. When I made an effort, she celebrated my trying. She appreciated every baby step I took. And she never hesitated to let me know when something didn't work or when there was room for improvement. Her honesty was useful because she provided me with specific examples of what I could do differently. She focused on my behavior, not on me as a person. She helped me identify alternative ways of behaving. But it was simply her willingness to tell me the truth that sent the greatest message.

And truth-telling is only one aspect of living honestly.

What does it mean to be dishonest? *Twelve Steps and Twelve Traditions* says, "It's the perverse wish to hide a bad motive underneath a good one." It further states, "This subtle and elusive kind of self-righteousness underlies the smallest act or thought." *As Bill Sees It* says, "The deception of others is almost always rooted in the deception of ourselves." Finally, *Alcoholics Anonymous* states, "Willingness, honesty and open mindedness are the essentials of recovery." How honest are you? Are you honest in certain situations? Does your level of honesty depend on who's involved? How much is at stake?

In a recent seminar that I facilitated, I used the example of the three political candidates. I then asked a group of forty people to discuss their views on honesty. The responses, from both the men and the women, were telling. The perspectives on honesty were as diverse as the group itself. I was surprised to discover that their level of honesty depended on a variety of factors, such as

1. whether the seminar participant had engaged in the behavior in question
2. whether a participant's friend or family member had engaged in the dishonest behavior
3. whether the activity involved someone the seminar participant liked
4. whether the person who engaged in the dishonest behavior said what the seminar participant wanted to hear, even if the person's actions weren't congruent with what he or she said

Here are some of the comments they made:

- "I can't believe he told the truth. He committed political suicide. I wouldn't do it."
- "He lied for the greater good. That makes it okay."

- "He did the right thing because he wants to win. You have to lie to win."
- "Honesty is when I don't lie, even if I don't exactly tell the truth."

Then they continued to share more broadly about the topic:

- "Honesty means not taking what's not mine. It doesn't matter whether it's sleeping with someone else's husband or boyfriend, taking drugs from their medicine cabinet, or stealing supplies from work."
- "Honesty is not getting caught."
- "It's okay to cheat on my taxes, I deserve it."
- "Honesty is telling the truth about my feelings, including when I hurt, even if I run the risk of being disliked."
- "Honesty is admitting when I'm wrong, even when I'm judged."
- "Honesty is being true to me. It's having the courage not to live a lie."

So even though we say we value honesty, why do we accept and sometimes encourage dishonesty? Because it's often easy, safe, and doesn't require much thought. Dishonesty is easier to justify if our role models aren't honest, the lie is about a seemingly small and unimportant thing, it's what we are accustomed to doing, or we are afraid not to lie.

Is there ever a time when honesty is not the best policy? You must be the judge. How far can you stretch your values and still live comfortably with yourself? Is it okay that I cheat on my taxes but not on my spouse? Is it okay that I take supplies from work but not money from a co-worker's wallet? Is it okay that I steal medicine from someone's medicine chest but not from my doctor? Is it okay that I lie about my feelings but insist my children tell the truth? What's my measure of honesty? And who's paying attention to the message I send when I live beyond my values? My kids? My students? My employees?

This week, you're invited to explore your level of honesty.

DAY 2

Define honesty. What does it mean to you? List four examples of honest behavior.

DAY 3

Today let's explore how subjective the concept of honesty can be. Consider this example: A man is married for ten years to a loving, dutiful, and caring wife. He begins an extramarital relationship with someone in his office. Is he dishonest? What if they were married for only six months? Would it matter? What if they were married for thirty-five years? What if the wife were pregnant? Disabled? What if the man were your best friend? Your father? You? What if you were the wife? The other woman? Is there really a subjective scale for honesty? Should there be?

DAY 4

As human beings, sometimes we don't tell the truth. Sometimes we cheat on taxes, tests, and relationships. Sometimes we are just afraid to be real. And for every time we are dishonest, stretch the truth, or interpret the truth in our favor, there's a payoff. There is always a payoff. Bring to mind a situation where you weren't honest in your dealings with another person. What was the payoff? And for every payoff, there is a price. What was yours?

DAY 5

Remember this quote: "It's the perverse wish to hide a bad motive underneath a good one." List two occasions when you hid a bad motive beneath a good one. Why did you? What was the payoff?

DAY 6

Describe what the following quotes mean to you: (1) "The deception of others is almost always rooted in the deception of ourselves."

(2) "Willingness, honesty and open mindedness are the essentials of recovery."

DAY 7

Today is your day to rest, recharge, regroup, and review your week. What observations can you make about your willingness to tell the truth? What worked? What didn't work? Was one day more challenging than another?

Act As If

Thought for the Week

Sometimes it's an esteemable act to act as if,
until you get it.

Affirmations for the Week

I accept the opportunity to act my way
into right living.

This week, I will act as if I am what I want to be.

Esteemable Actions for the Week

DAY 1

"Acting as if" is a powerful tool for successful living. It is one that, when properly applied, renders triumphant and bountiful results. The idea that we can believe one thing, yet take contrary action and get positive results, is remarkable. Think about it. How often have you given up on something simply because you didn't believe you could have it or do it? Yet on the contrary, how often have you accomplished a goal because you were willing to do the work, even though deep in your heart you never believed you could do it?

It's sweet when the path we take is trouble free. When there are no challenges, no glitches, no obstructions to getting from one place to another. It's nice when we can move in and out of experiences with grace and ease. Indeed, when we believe we can do something, it's easy to do. No doubt it's our confidence that propels us to the next level. And confidence, at times, is a wonderful trait.

But what about when we want to create a different experience in our lives, but we don't quite believe we can do it? What about when we lack the confidence, which is merely a belief that we will succeed? Does that mean we have no chance of doing well, simply because we don't think we can? Some people will have us believe that that's true. They suggest that in order to make it at anything, we absolutely must believe we can. To back up that theory, there are countless authors, therapists, lecturers, and others who tell us that confidence is the precursor to success. And without it, we won't make it.

I must disagree. If that were true, I and many others wouldn't be where we are today.

I didn't get through law school because I believed in myself. I wish I could say that I did. For sure, there were moments of feeling that "Yes, I can do this. Yes, I'm making it happen. Yes, it's a piece of cake." But there were many more moments of feeling that "I can't, it's hard, and I want to give up." My classmates all seemed to be confident. Perhaps they were. For me, the best I could do was to be fully present. In my mind, it didn't matter what I thought as long as I was willing to show up for class, do my homework, hand in term papers, and get passing grades. What I had, and continue to have, going for me is a willingness to do the work—even when I don't believe I'll make it to the finish line.

Sometimes we get caught up thinking we have to feel good each and every moment on the journey. That life has to be easy and uncomplicated or else it's not worth living. How often do we hear it said that "life doesn't have to be hard"? On some level that's true, depending on the choices we make. If we make safe and easy choices that don't stretch us or test our growth, then we may have easy lives. But if we're doing anything that is new, different, or outside of our comfort zone, there will be days we'll feel great and days when we'll struggle just to get out of bed. Acting as if is the key. A willingness to take contrary action enabled me to change my reality, simply because I moved my feet. Even today when I set out to get a certain result, I don't always believe I'll get what I want. There are no guarantees. My job is simply to do the work and act as if. The rest is up to my Higher Power.

Some of you might think acting as if is being phony, because you're doing something you don't believe in. And perhaps you're right. But how often do we fake it in our lives with no purposeful goal other than to impress someone? Why not "fake it until we make it" as we move ourselves closer to completing our goal? We're just practicing doing what we say we want to do. We're strengthening our spiritual muscles by acting as if we're already doing what we want to do. We're affirming our mental reality. Do the footwork and the mind will follow. It's all in how we see it.

This week, you're invited to examine the spiritual tool of acting as if to help you realize your goals, and to consider the opportunities you have in your life to do so.

DAY 2

People either buy into the concept of acting as if or they don't. Being unwilling to see its benefits can create blocks in your mind. So today, let's examine your thinking about acting in a way that's contrary to the way you feel. Without giving it too much thought, write down the first six words that come to your mind when you think about the following concepts:

- acting as if
- contrary action
- take the action and the mind will follow

Some of your words may be positive, some not. Next to each positive word, write down the old belief that would have stopped you from getting into action. If it's a negative word, write down a new word that will get you into acting as if.

DAY 3

Identify three or four incomplete tasks or activities in your life where you can practice acting as if.

DAY 4

Today let's practice acting as if. If you sit back and wait to be in the mood to do something, you'll probably be waiting for a long time. Bring to mind an important task you need to complete that you'd rather not do. What act-as-if actions can you take to get the job done? Do one.

DAY 5

Identify three ways you can incorporate acting as if into your daily spiritual practice. Do one thing today.

DAY 6

What have you been putting off doing this week? Maybe you've been looking at that pile of laundry sitting in the corner, perhaps your car needs to be washed, maybe the cat needs to be combed, perhaps you've put off going to the gym, or maybe you've said, "Just one more puff, and then I'll stop smoking." Whatever it is, today is your day to act as if you are someone who follows through.

DAY 7

Finally, today is your day to rest, recharge, regroup, and review your week. What observations can you make about your willingness to act as if? Was it more of a challenge than you thought it would be? Why? What day seemed extra hard?

Accountability

Thought for the Week

Self-esteem comes from taking responsibility
for your choices.

Affirmations for the Week

I am accountable for the choices I make.

This week, I will choose wisely.

Esteemable Actions for the Week

DAY 1

Once in an interview, I was asked, "What is the secret to your success?"

"Continued sobriety, a strong belief in a God that works under all conditions, a fabulous recovery support system over the years, treasured mentors, my mother, a loving husband, and a willingness to do the work" I responded. "But the two most important factors," I said, "have been my courageous spirit and my willingness to be accountable for my actions."

Each time I did something I was afraid to do, I was a winner. Going back to school, becoming a lawyer, continuing to take the Bar exam after multiple failures, letting go of the practice of law, asking for help, revealing my story publicly, and speaking up against injustice, particularly when I feared retaliation, have all been opportunities to walk through my fear.

I am also willing to be held accountable for the choices, actions, and decisions I make. Accountability is a point of view that is practiced through action. It means looking at the part we play in everything that happens to us. It means seeing ourselves as volunteers and participants in our lives, not as victims of circumstances. This is a difficult mind-set to master, particularly when we don't like what's happening. But once we get in the habit of seeing our part, we profit in many ways, such as the following:

1. You get greater results because you're focused on solutions. Victims wait for things to change to feel better. Accountable people take charge and recognize what they can do now.

2. You feel more empowered because you're more in control. When you're not sitting around waiting for something to happen, you feel good and in control of your life.

3. You genuinely feel better about yourself because you make healthier choices. There is a sense of self-esteem that results from making right choices.

4. You make different choices because you know you'll be held responsible.

5. You are smarter because you learn from your mistakes. It's less likely you'll repeat them.

As far back as I can remember, I've seen myself as a victim. Someone who got sucked up by life. My alcoholism, my addiction, my bad choices in men, and my lifestyle as a young adult were all someone else's fault. It was my mother's fault. She burped me the wrong way, she was too hard on me, she was too lenient, she cared too much or not enough. Had she been a better parent, I would have turned out differently. Or it was my father's fault. Had he been there for me, I would not have sought relief in the arms of older men. Or it was those men who made me do things I didn't want to do. Then, of course, it was my boss, the Bar exam, my cats. When that didn't work, I could always resort to the old standby: I'm black, I'm a woman, and I have a colorful past. I was just a hapless victim of circumstances.

There were a lot of reasons why I acted as I did, but none satisfactorily excused my behavior. Instead, those reasons only explained my behavior. Undeniably, growing up poor, female, and black in America affected the way I saw things and, to some degree, influenced my behavior. But like it or not, fair or unfair, in each and every case, I made the ultimate decisions about my fate. My unwillingness to see my part kept me stuck for years; my life changed when I owned my part in what happened.

We get support in being victims and seeing ourselves as victims. When I made poor choices and was faced with the consequences of those choices, often there was someone to step in and clean up my mess. There was no incentive to stop the unhealthy behavior if I never had to pay a price. I was also told things like "It's not your fault," "If they hadn't done what they did, you would have behaved differently," "You couldn't help yourself," or my personal favorite, "You're an alcoholic, that's why you did it." As if being an alcoholic gave me permission to behave in any way I wanted. There was always an escape route available. And I used it.

Accountability is a choice we make and a process that never ends. This week, you're invited to discover and uncover behaviors that keep you stuck in blame, and you're invited to identify opportunities for greater accountability and thereby greater self-esteem.

DAY 2

Identify one personal success you've had. It can be related to work, school, home, community, or family. What did it take for you to succeed? What attitudes, behaviors, and beliefs helped you reach your goal?

DAY 3

Now bring to mind a situation that didn't quite turn out as you wanted. What happened? Was there anything you could have done differently? Were there red flags you chose to ignore? Was there help available you didn't seek out?

DAY 4

Thinking back on your experience mentioned in day 3, what behaviors contributed to your lack of success? How long did you allow the outcome to bother you? Are you still holding on to what happened? If so, why? If so, do you see a correlation between your unsuccessful attempt and your attitude?

DAY 5

Today think about a situation you're currently involved in where you're not pleased with the way it's playing out. Is there something you can do to change the course of events? Are there signals you can respond to now? Is there help you can get? What proactive steps can you take?

DAY 6

Today think further about opportunities for greater accountability. What's happening in your life that, if you were to shift your thinking, might evolve differently?

DAY 7

Today is your day to rest, recharge, regroup, and review your week. What observations can you make about your willingness to be accountable? What worked? What didn't work? Was one day more challenging than another?

WEEK 44

Just Show Up

Thought for the Week

It's an esteemable act to show up,
especially when you don't want to.

Affirmations for the Week

This week, I will show up for myself
or someone else.

This week, I will put one foot in front of the
other and just show up.

Esteemable Actions for the Week

DAY 1

It was so hard to get out of bed that morning. I was still feeling the
effects of the day before. My body ached as if I had been beaten up
physically, but I was just emotionally assaulted. I thought to myself,
"Stop fighting and give yourself permission to hang out and do
nothing today. Use today to lie on the couch and watch videos or
old reruns on television." While the idea sounded good, and no
doubt there were days when I put that suggestion into practice,
today was not that day.

On my calendar were appointments, meetings, and tasks that
needed attending to. It was a day in which the scheduled events

couldn't be postponed or cancelled without dire consequences. It was the kind of day that demanded that no matter how I felt, I still had to show up. And show up I did.

Why should you show up when you don't want to? There are any number of reasons, all of which speak to personal responsibility and self-esteem. When you show up, particularly if you don't want to, here are the benefits:

1. You get results. Suppose you decide to learn to use a computer because it would increase your productivity at work and position you for a better raise. You take three of the ten classes and you're ready to give up. It's much harder than you thought it would be, and you don't have time to bother. While you can always stop taking the classes, the benefits of continuing are great: increased productivity, a raise, and a new marketable skill you can take anywhere.

2. You gain the satisfaction of follow-through. It's easy to give up; it's hard to follow through and stay the course. Your gift to yourself is that you followed through on something you started. You kept your agreement to yourself.

3. You become known as someone who can be counted on to do what you say you'll do. Not only do you see yourself as someone who can be counted on, other people see you as someone who lives with integrity.

4. You get increased self-esteem. Self-esteem comes from doing esteemable acts; it's an esteemable act to do what you say you'll do and to show up when you don't want to.

5. You gain an inner strength that comes from doing the hard work. Something magical happens when you tackle a tough problem and get to the other side—you get stronger. While problems may not seem to get easier, you become more adept at handling them.

6. You get an opportunity to be of service. The best teachers and guides are those who have been through the fire, reached the other side, and are willing to share their experience, strength, and hope with others.

This week is your opportunity to practice some tips that can help you through your next bad stretch of time.

DAY 2

Think of a situation you want to let go of. Maybe it's a project you've started, a test you've taken and failed, a course you've attempted to study, a book you've made an effort to read, a relationship you've entered into, or anything else. Bring to mind that situation and write about it today. Why are you ready to give up on it?

DAY 3

Make a pros and cons list. What would you gain from staying the course? Imagine what awaits you on the other side, such as a better job, a healthier relationship, a college degree, the completion of a process. Now think about the payoff of giving up. What are the benefits of not staying the course? Sometimes it might actually be the best thing to do, and sometimes it might not.

DAY 4

What would it take for you to follow through on your commitment? Is there someone you can go to for help? Is there someone who can assist you or support you through the process? Is there another resource you can utilize? Is there an easy-to-use manual you can purchase or a course that will help you?

DAY 5

Today break your big task into small pieces. List all the steps within the bigger task that you can take. For example, if your big task is to prepare for a test by reading a two-hundred-page manual, you could break it down into baby-step pieces as follows:

- Identify how much time you have before the test.
- Identify how many pages in total you need to read.

- Determine whether there is a practice exam you can take prior to the real test.
- After you've determined how far you are from the test date and how much material you must review, assign a number of pages to read per day, week, or month.
- Schedule your study time, including exactly what you'll read on what day.

DAY 6

Just show up and do something!

DAY 7

Today is your day to rest, recharge, regroup, and review your week. What observations can you make about your willingness to show up? How hard was it for you this week to do what you didn't want to do? Was there a day that worked best for you? What didn't work?

WEEK
45

Change Your Thinking, Change Your Life

Thought for the Week

It's an esteemable act to let go of ideas
that no longer work.

Affirmations for the Week

I am open to new ideas.

This week, I will act as if I believe
in the impossible.

Esteemable Actions for the Week

DAY 1

Above, you'll see a new idea for a bouncing ball. Before moving ahead with the reading, take a moment and list four to five observations, remarks, or comments about the new idea for the ball. What are your thoughts? Now I'd like you to categorize each of your comments, observations, and remarks by placing a "+" next to the positive comments, a "-" next to the negative comments, and a "0" next to the neutral comments.

When I recently gave this same exercise to a seminar group, they responded as follows:

"That's not a ball, it's a bowling pin."

"That's a strange-looking ball."

"It can't roll. It's not round."

"There's a handle, and balls don't have handles."

"What kind of ball is that?"

"That's a stupid idea for a ball."

"How can we make it into a ball?"

"What would it take to get it to roll?"

Of the above comments, only two could be perceived as positive or solution-focused. What this illustrates is how we react to things we see as different, particularly when they appear unusual or odd. Undeniably, if we look at the above picture as a traditional ball, it doesn't work. But if we see it in terms of possibilities, it can.

It's easy to get caught up in seeing the world through a narrow lens. It's easy to limit ourselves to what we already know and believe. But what would happen if we challenged our beliefs and stretched? What would happen if we changed our thinking to accommodate a belief in endless possibilities? What would happen if we were able to see the possibilities in the ball pictured above? What would happen if we were able to see the possibilities in our own lives?

What do you believe about yourself? Imagine believing the following about yourself:

- I am worthy of love.
- I am a good person.
- I can live in a violence-free home.
- I can live the life I want.
- I won't die if I speak my truth.
- I can operate a computer.

- I am healthy.
- I live in an abundant universe.
- I can stop the madness in my life.

And what if you really believed those things to be true: how would you act?

- I would choose wisely.
- I could be anything I want to be.
- I would pass that test I'm afraid to take.
- I would be a nonsmoker.
- I would be a nondrinker.
- I would live an abundant life.
- I would say no to inappropriate behavior.

What if those things and so much more could really be true? How would you act if you were loved, successful, living the life you want to live? You have the power to see the world through a new pair of glasses. Not that the old ones don't work, because they do to some extent—they've brought you here. But sometimes our old glasses become ineffective because our vision changes, we age and get wiser, or sometimes the glasses simply become dirty from daily use. Sometimes we just need a new pair of glasses to provide us with a fresh perspective.

So how do we change our thinking? Here are a few suggestions:

- Think in terms of possibilities. What if you choose to believe you can do, be, have, and feel any way you want?
- Ask yourself, "How would I need to behave if it were true? How would I act if I believed in endless possibilities?"
- Focus on solutions. You may tend to immediately go to the negative when you encounter something that's new and different. If a task seems impossible, ask yourself, "What would it take to make it happen? What would I need to do? How would I need to be?"
- Let go of your need to be right. Perhaps at first blush, the idea

seems silly, ridiculous, impracticable, or totally unattainable. So what? You may be right. But what if you are wrong?

- Listen with an open heart. You may often listen with half an ear, waiting for the opportunity to judge, condemn, and criticize an idea. Consider listening for understanding.

This week, you're invited to stretch your mind, expand your thinking, and enlarge your vision to believe that anything is possible. And if you believe that anything is possible, how would you behave?

DAY 2

As you go through this day, become aware of your tendency to criticize new and unusual ideas. Be particularly mindful of how quickly you say, "No," "That's silly," "That's not a ball," or something similar, before having all the information. Bring to mind how you responded to the picture of the ball.

DAY 3

As you read through the list in day 1, which had the greatest effect on you? Why? How would you behave if you really believed those things to be true?

DAY 4

Bring to mind a situation that you have criticized or judged harshly. What tools can you use to change your thinking?

DAY 5

Go back to the example of the bouncing ball. Next to each of your observations, comments, or remarks, substitute a solution-oriented statement, such as the following:

OLD IDEA: "It can't roll. It's not round."
NEW IDEA: "Since the sides are rounded, it can roll on its side."

DAY 6

Sometimes the words we use to describe things send a subtle message of judgment. Today be aware of the language you use to describe anything. Make a list of judgmental, critical, or even abusive words you use to describe an experience or respond to an idea someone shared with you.

DAY 7

Today is your day to rest, recharge, regroup, and review your week. What observations can you make about your thinking? Your quickness to respond in a critical, negative, or abusive manner? What lessons did you learn this week? What action will you carry into the next week?

WEEK 46

Ask for What You Need

Thought for the Week

Self-esteem comes from having the courage
to ask for what you need and want.

Affirmations for the Week

I am ready to ask for what I need and want.

This week, I will ask for what I need
to take care of myself.

Esteemable Actions for the Week

DAY 1

It was 6:30 in the morning and I was in McCarran Airport waiting for my flight to return home. I was hungry and didn't want to risk eating something on the plane that I'd regret. So I scouted around the concourse for some possible options. I approached the first food counter and asked for what I wanted, even though I didn't see it on the menu. I've learned that it's better to ask, even if you don't see what you want, because they just might have it. So I asked. The server was really kind and said, "It's good that you asked. Even though it's not on today's menu, we usually have it." He continued, "You might check the restaurant next door."

"Thank you," I said, and I went next door.

Again, I didn't see what I wanted on the menu but decided that I'd at least ask. The worst thing they could say would be "Sorry, we don't have it." I walked up to the counter and asked for my selection.

"Do you see it on the menu?" the server said, in a somewhat irritated tone.

"No," I said, "but sometimes it's worth a shot to ask."

He said, "Not here. You get what you see and we don't make 'egg white' anything. This is not a gourmet restaurant."

"Do you have oatmeal?" I asked, in an effort not to give up on my food plan.

"No, we don't have oatmeal. Is there anything *on* the menu you'd like?"

"No, thank you," I said, and I left.

As I walked away, I overheard him saying to a co-worker, "Some people are so picky. She should eat what she can get. Everybody's on a health kick today."

Some of you might be thinking if I had asked for something on the menu, this would have never happened. And you know, you're right. But at that moment in time, I wanted what worked for my meal plan. I didn't want bacon, fried eggs, and hash browns; I wanted a healthier choice.

How many of us give up too soon or don't even ask for what we need because we're afraid someone will perceive us as "high maintenance" and picky, with an ungrateful attitude, because our health needs differ from theirs? How many of us make a choice every day not to take care of our needs because someone might not like us? For years I was that person. The one who couldn't or wouldn't ask for what she needed for fear of what others would think. Today I'm not.

It's no mistake that each week this book addresses fear in some way. A powerful force, fear defines who we are, controls the choices we make, and keeps us stuck in places we'd rather not be.

How do we learn to ask for what we want?

1. Know going into a situation that it probably won't be easy. You're doing something you're not used to doing.
2. Just ask. You'll never know unless you ask. I can't tell you how many opportunities I missed simply because I was afraid to ask for what I needed or wanted.
3. Know that there will be times you'll get what you want, and times you won't. Sometimes I get what I want when I want it; sometimes I don't. That's life, and I've got to live with it.
4. Have a plan B. Be prepared in case you don't get what you want. Are there alternatives you can live with? Is there another option?
5. What can you do in the future to be better prepared for similar circumstances? In my particular case, I can perhaps bring snacks with me or eat a little something before I leave for the airport. Think of alternatives that work for you.

This week, you're invited to ask for what you need and want in a variety of situations.

DAY 2

Think of a situation in the last week where you didn't ask for something you needed or wanted. Perhaps it was asking for a particular kind of food on a restaurant's menu, asking for a well-deserved raise, asking for your spouse or partner to listen to something you needed to say, or asking for respect from someone you felt hadn't given it to you. Whatever it is, write a paragraph about that situation.

DAY 3

Today let's explore why you weren't able to ask for what you needed or wanted. What stood in your way? If it was a form of fear, write in detail exactly what you were afraid of. If you see it as something else, explain in detail.

DAY 4

Today let's start asking. Let's begin with something relatively easy. I say "relatively" because what might appear easy to one person is by no means easy to another. Select an easy task for you. Maybe it's asking the grocery store attendant for something you want that you don't see on the shelf. Maybe it's asking your kids or your husband to pick up around the house.

DAY 5

Today we'll ask for something with higher stakes. Perhaps it's asking for what you really want on a menu. For example, maybe you like well-done steak. But you've always been afraid to ask for it because, when you were growing up, your father told you it was a waste of a good piece of meat to cook it well done. Today is your day to ask. Or if a server brings you something you don't want, ask him or her to correct it. Perhaps you are deserving of a long-overdue raise, and you have enough documentation to show you deserve it. Today is your day to ask for it.

DAY 6

Today we ask for a little more, and today's task goes right to the heart of what we fear: that we won't be liked. Today ask for something you need and want but have been afraid to ask for all week or longer. Maybe it's asking someone to stop talking to you in a disrespectful manner. Maybe it's the issue on day 2, and now at day 6, you know in your heart you need to go for it. Today is your day to summon up the courage and ask.

DAY 7

Finally, today is your day to rest, recharge, regroup, and review your week. What observations can you make about your willingness to ask for what you need or want? Was it more of a challenge than you thought it would be? Why? What day seemed extra hard?

WEEK 47

Love Is an Action

Thought for the Week

It's an esteemable act to show love through action.

Affirmations for the Week

I am willing to show love for myself
and others through action.

This week, I will act my way into self-love.

Esteemable Actions for the Week

DAY 1

Love is an action word. It goes beyond the words to the doing. It's the behavior behind the words that make the concept of loving come alive. Think about it. How often have you said something with your words, but your attitude, facial expression, and behavior said something different? How often has someone said "I love you" to you, but his or her behavior spoke something utterly different? When you love people, you treat them in a way that shows you care about, cherish, treasure, respect, and honor them. And charity begins at home.

How easy it is to say you love yourself, yet treat your mind, body, and spirit with disrespect, or allow others to do the same. If love is really an action word, how do you express self-love? Some people believe standing in front of the mirror repeating "I love me" is an expression of self-love. Others believe if you wear beautiful, stylish, and expensive clothes, you love yourself. Still others buy into the notion that if you live in the right neighborhood, are attached to the right person, send your kids to the right school, have the right credentials behind your name, or drive the right car, you show the world how much you love yourself. If that were the case, every rich person would feel good about who he or she is.

This book suggests that self-love starts with having the courage to be ourselves, under all conditions—to not compromise who we are in order to be liked by others. How easy it is to live a lie, live as others would have you live, at whatever the cost. One of my uncles died young. He was only forty-three. While he knew he was gay for many years, he never quite came to terms with who he was. He allowed other people to define him. It didn't work. Now he's dead.

Self-love is having the courage to live our dreams and do what makes us happy in life, so that we don't wake up one day and say, "I wish I would have . . ." Self-love is about practicing self-care and making our health a priority. It's hard to say we love ourselves when we don't take care of our health, which includes eating properly, exercising, and maintaining emotional balance. When we love ourselves, we're willing to set boundaries and protect them, knowing that "no" is a complete sentence all by itself. When we love ourselves, we're willing to make agreements with ourselves and keep them. Self-love is demonstrated in the choices we make in relationships, money management, and careers. Indeed, self-love is very much about the things we do, more than about the things we say.

How we describe ourselves speaks to our level of self-love. Negative self-talk is one of the most destructive behaviors we engage in, because after a while, we start to believe what we say. It often begins with describing ourselves in a derogatory way, using words such as *stupid, idiot, dummy,* or *worthless.* After a while, we become desensitized to those words, and they simply become a working part of our vocabulary. Then before we know it, by our actions, we give others permission to call us names.

Another way we demonstrate self-love is having the courage not to settle for seconds in jobs or relationships. How many of you reading this are stuck in jobs that no longer work (or never have), yet you haven't left? How many of you are tolerating abuse of any kind in your relationship, yet you continually make excuses for staying? Abuse is not just physical; it's mental and emotional as well. For example, allowing someone to talk to you in any way they want is submitting to emotional abuse, as is allowing your cheating partner to consistently return to your bed. Choosing to ignore your partner's affairs is not an act of self-love. Yes, there may be valid reasons for staying—temporarily—such as financial support, the kids, or not having somewhere else to go. But overcoming those obstacles should be your priority, not staying. There are always reasons for staying in unhealthy relationships and jobs, but after a while, the excuses stop working and you're challenged to take action on your own behalf or on behalf of your kids.

Finally, we provide evidence of our real love of self when we have the courage to speak up. Sometimes we're afraid to speak up because we don't think we have anything important to say. Sometimes we're afraid people won't want to hear what we have to say. Sometimes we're afraid of being judged. Sometimes we're afraid of the conflict that is sure to arise when we say what we feel. Having the courage to speak up, regardless of the perceived outcome, is an esteemable act. One thing to remember: how you speak up is as important as what you say. We don't have a right to be hurtful toward others simply because we want to share our feelings. Be tactful and kind.

This week, you're invited to practice some new behaviors.

DAY 2

In what ways are you not being yourself? How can you live more authentically, more in alignment with who you really are? What stops you?

DAY 3

Today list the negative words you use to describe yourself, your thoughts, and your feelings. Why do you use those words to describe yourself, your thoughts, and your feelings? Now, replace each word with a more positive description of yourself. The way to really change how you talk about yourself is to practice using the new words. Practice using the new words and phrases.

DAY 4

Make a list of the jobs you've had during the last five years. What did you like about each one? What did you not like? What about your present job? Do you enjoy what you do? Why? If not, why not? Why do you stay in a job you hate? What's the payoff? How does staying in a job you don't like move you further from self-love?

DAY 5

Now turn your attention to your relationships. List the most important ones, perhaps those with a spouse, parent, teacher, mentor, boss, or friend. Describe each relationship. What works, and what doesn't? When you are with this person or talking to him or her on the phone, how do you feel? What esteemable actions are you willing to take to make it a better relationship for yourself?

DAY 6

Recall three to five times you wish you had spoken up, starting with today. How could you have handled a situation differently? Was there an opportunity for you to speak up? Was there something that needed to be said that you didn't say in the moment?

DAY 7

Today is your day to rest, recharge, regroup, and review your week. What observations can you make about your willingness to practice new and different behaviors? What worked for you this week? What didn't? Was one day more challenging than another? How?

Angels Are Everywhere

Thought for the Week

Self-esteem comes from appreciating people
who have helped you along the way.

Affirmations for the Week

I see angels everywhere.
This week, I will say thank you to my angels.

Esteemable Actions for the Week

DAY 1

I never believed in angels. Now I do. I think of angels as people who do nice things for us without expecting much in return. They give for the love of giving. They seek out opportunities to help, even when it seems inconvenient. They don't always look like we expect them to look or smell like we think they should. Their beliefs aren't always aligned with ours. But when we need them, they are there.

One of the first times I really understood this concept was when I drove to New York from Las Vegas in 1982. There I was, with just two years of driving experience, in my 1981 Mustang with my two scared kitties, Jason and Athena, and a U-Haul trailer. The journey was complete with torrential rainstorms, hours and hours of barren desert, and big trucks that always had the right of way. There I was, thrust into a big world I had never known except in geography schoolbooks. I was terrified but willing to make the drive. This cross-country trip was to become a metaphor for the bigger journey in my life.

I had done my homework for six months: finding maps, assessing my travel distance, getting meeting schedules, securing hotel reservations, identifying places to eat, preparing the cats with vaccinations and medication, praying, gathering phone numbers, and getting my car ready for the long drive ahead. With all that preparation, there were still opportunities for angels to do their work with me. And work they did.

Angels were everywhere. I met them in gas stations and rest stops, on the highway, in hotels, at restaurants, and at every meeting place I stopped along the way. From Flagstaff, Arizona, to Albuquerque, New Mexico, from Joplin, Missouri, to Chicago, Illinois, and then on to New York. Their support was unfailing. Because of them, I got from one city to another. Because of them, I completed my journey. My job was simply to show up; they did the rest.

When was the last time you recognized an angel? Perhaps they let your car pass into the next lane without giving you a dirty look. Maybe they were in the car ahead of you and paid your bridge or tunnel toll. Perhaps they offered to assist you when you were overloaded with bags. Maybe they helped you up instead of walking by when you fell on the stairs. Perhaps they gave you their seat on the subway or the bus. Maybe they gave you a gift they knew you'd like. Perhaps they loaned you some money, bought clothes or toys for your kids when you couldn't, or just lent a helping hand in whatever way they could. Or maybe it was a friend who just stopped in the middle of a busy workday to take your call or meet with you for coffee or lunch. An angel can be someone you know or someone you meet in passing. Angels enhance your life, if even for a moment.

Why aren't we aware of the angels in our lives? Sometimes we're just too busy to stop to see who's helping us. We are so unintentionally caught up in our day-to-day affairs that we don't notice a kindness has been done. Sometimes we are purposefully self-centered and we just don't care. Sometimes our sense of entitlement makes us arrogantly believe people should automatically help us, simply because of who we are. Regardless of the reason, when we fail to appreciate people who have been there for us, we and they lose out.

Why are angels so important? Why are they a necessary part of our experience? They make the world a better place. They open up our heart and warm our soul. They remind us that people are good and kind and that the need to help others is a part of the human spirit. Without them, we think we can do things all by ourselves. We give them opportunities to be of service. They have lessons to learn. We have lessons to learn. They teach us we can be even better then we already are. Their work provides a benchmark at which we can aim.

This week, you're invited to recognize and acknowledge the angels in your life, people who have contributed to your life in big and small ways.

DAY 2

Let's begin by identifying the angels of your past. Think back over your life and bring into consciousness the faces of people who have been there for you. In some cases, they might not even be in your life today. Maybe one was your best friend from junior high school or high school. Maybe one was the owner of the corner candy store or the school bus driver. Maybe one was your neighbor or your best friend's mom who inspired, motivated, challenged, or supported you into doing something you didn't think you could do. Sometimes your most ardent supporters have been sweet and kind, and sometimes they've motivated you through tough love. Consider the following as part of your list: parents, grandparents, stepparents, adoptive parents, a spouse, former spouses, aunts, uncles, teachers,

counselors, coaches, therapists, friends, estranged friends, employ-
ers, co-workers, or neighborhood retailers. Identify as many as you
can and don't beat up on yourself if you can't come up with anyone.
Just do your best.

DAY 3

Next to each person on your gratitude list, write what you're grateful
for. Allow yourself to really think through this exercise. The thing
you're most grateful for may lie underneath the surface. After you've
written your answers, go back and review them, just in case there is
something more you want to add.

DAY 4

Today I'd like you to make your gratitude list more current. List the
people in your life today who are there for you. Consider people beyond the obvious ones. Sometimes it helps if you think of the act of
kindness first and then attach a name or face to the deed, such as
the computer guy who helped you get rid of your virus, the co-
worker who covered for you when you were late for a meeting, or
the person who takes care of your animals.

DAY 5

The next step is to write a gratitude letter to someone on your list.
In some cases, this will be an enjoyable experience and the words
will flow from your heart. You'll be happy someone gave you permission to put on paper what you feel. In other cases, you'll feel
challenged, particularly if the person is no longer in your life, if you
love the person but have never told him or her so, if the person is
someone who has also hurt you, or if you just don't know the right
words to say. Write a rough draft. Just get started. There is no perfect first draft. Stay in your heart as much as you can. Your mind
should only play a part when remembering the specific things this
person has done for you. Then let your heart take over. At times like

these, prayer works for me in being open to the right words and divine guidance. Rework the letter at least five times until its words and tone are right. After you've revised it a few times, share it with a close friend for a "feeling and tone" review.

DAY 6

The final step is contact. In some cases you'll know exactly how to reach the person. For others, you may have to search. Depending on who it is, how long it has been since you last connected, or what the circumstances were, you will need to exercise caution before taking that final step. Don't go forging ahead to find someone who might not want to be found. Honor his or her boundaries. It's important that you not make yourself feel better at someone else's expense. So tread lightly, but take some action. Get started!

DAY 7

Once again, today you're invited to rest, recharge, regroup, and review your week. What observations can you make about your behavior this week? Was acknowledging angels in your life helpful? Was one day especially rewarding? Painful?

Make Time for the Connection

Thought for the Week

Self-esteem comes from making time
to connect with others.

Affirmations for the Week

I am open to making the connection.

This week, I will make time to connect
with people I love.

Esteemable Actions for the Week

DAY 1

In our ever-changing, fast-paced, disposable culture, it's difficult to really bond with one another. There was a time when we were more connected, when we actually met for coffee instead of sending e-mails. Now we don't have time to be with our kids, eat a meal with a friend, or visit our parents. We don't have time to smile at someone passing by us on the street. We don't have time to make the connection it takes to live comfortably in our skin. We're just too busy making money or doing whatever seems to be more important in the moment. I'm not suggesting those things are not important, because indeed, they are. But somewhere along the road, we've lost our connection to each other. It might help to get it back.

I'm better now, but I, too, have been guilty of not making time for loved ones. For years I said my friends and family were important, but rarely did I make the time to connect with them. Sure, on occasion I ran in for a quick "Hi, how are you," then ran off, but a real connection was missing. A number of years ago, I was traveling to New York six to eight times a year. Each time I'd call my mother and suggest having lunch. I can only recall maybe one or two times when we actually saw one another during that period. I'd call on my way out of town to say, once again, "I'm sorry, Mama, I got tied up." Fortunately my mother had a busy life of her own and appeared to be understanding. But even so, after so many cancellations, even the most tolerant and patient person reaches the limit.

And technology doesn't help. Many of us are more connected to things than we are to people. Cell phones, e-mail, computers, and faxes provide us with easier, smarter, and faster ways to communicate with each other, without ever bringing us face to face. These tools may make our lives easier and more efficient, but they remove the opportunity for intimacy. Further, technology gives us a venue to say things in ways we wouldn't dream of doing face to face. Why? Because we can't see the person. Think of how often we feel it's okay to leave a rude message in an e-mail or voice mail.

Technology is wonderful and enables us to stay in touch, but when it becomes a substitute for a real connection, we have a problem. There are times when I absolutely can't see someone because I don't live nearby or because it's more challenging to connect in person. In that case, the telephone is the next best thing. Then, on those occasions when the telephone doesn't work, e-mail is acceptable. But whenever possible, the nearer we are to one another, the better. And when we do communicate, really *being connected* is important. Being as fully present on the phone as we would be in person is a sign that we value the connection. Sometimes technology allows us to be present without really being present. When we're on the phone, for example, and no one can see us, it's easy to have our attention elsewhere, such as on our computer screen.

Connection is not just about making time for family and friends. It's about a sense of caring for other people. It's about connecting with the human spirit even when there is no national crisis. The other day I was walking down the street when a woman ahead of me tripped and fell on the sidewalk. Two people walked by her as if she weren't there. Others just stared without offering help. I stopped to help, as did another person. We both waited for an ambulance to arrive, and then we left. I couldn't believe what I had just witnessed: a human being was in need of assistance and most people walked on by.

If we give lip service to love, if we say we are connected as Americans, how can we not be kind to the individuals we meet along our journey, regardless of their race, gender, religion, or sexual orientation? What happened to the connection?

This week is about making the connection. It's about making the time to connect with others.

DAY 2

Have you been remiss at connecting with someone in your coterie of friends? Who? Perhaps it's a friend in another state, or a friend right around the corner.

DAY 3

Make the connection. It might simply be to schedule a meal or a walk or a playdate for the kids. If you can't meet, schedule a phone call.

DAY 4

Don't stop there. Who else have you not connected with in a while? Maybe you don't have time for a face-to-face meeting, but what about a phone call? Who on your list would love to hear from you?

Just a quick "Hello, I'm thinking about you" can make somebody's day. Maybe you're not in the mood to do it for yourself, but think about how someone else will be pleased by your generous effort. Last week I called an uncle I hadn't spoken to in years. I was happy I made the call, and he was really thrilled to hear from me. It was a small gesture, but a kind gesture. Make somebody's day.

DAY 5

So, okay, maybe you really don't have the time for even a phone call because it might turn into a lengthy adventure. Then try dropping someone an e-mail saying "Just thinking of you." There are wonderful e-card companies with cute electronic cards to choose from. Why not send someone a card today?

DAY 6

Is there anyone else you think would love to hear from you this week? Make the connection. Don't let the day go by without connecting with another human being. Also, what about extending yourself to someone you wouldn't normally reach out to? Perhaps it's someone at work, someone at the gym, or someone you see in the elevator every day but never speak to. You might stop to connect with the person who serves you coffee, the person who helps you with your bags at the airport, the bus driver, the subway conductor, the parking attendant, your housekeeper, or the guy in the supermarket. Whoever it is, make the connection today.

DAY 7

Once again, today you're invited to rest, recharge, regroup, and review your week. What observations can you make about your willingness to connect with others in your sphere? Outside your sphere? Was one day more difficult than another? Why?

WEEK 50

Being Prepared

Thought for the Week

Self-esteem comes from having a consciousness
of preparedness.

Affirmations for the Week

I can be prepared.

This week, I will prepare for what's ahead.

Esteemable Actions for the Week

DAY 1

What does it mean to be prepared? It means to be ready, to be equipped in whatever way is required for the experience at hand. In some situations, that means being rested and not running on empty. In other situations, it means having studied for an exam, prepped for a speech, or checked our equipment and materials prior to a presentation. In still other situations, being prepared means having what it takes to handle a problem effectively.

Why is it important to be prepared? It makes our lives easier. There is less stress because we are equipped to handle unexpected problems and we've allotted extra time in case we need it. We feel good about our work because we were able to think through all the details and plan for potential obstacles. Being prepared gives us a chance to step back—with room to spare—and assess the situation. If preparing for a talk, meeting, or program, being ready in advance allows us to schmooze with the audience and build rapport rather than studying our material at the last minute. There is less time spent on working through a problem or cleaning up a mess because we've already run through the "what if" scenarios.

Yet for all the benefits of preparedness, many people still see it as a time-consuming waste. Lack of planning is more about our beliefs than about our lack of time. Here are a few beliefs that keep us from being better prepared for the events in our lives:

1. If you're busy (or appear busy), you must be important.
2. Planning takes too much time on the front end.
3. Planning is a waste of time.
4. Even if you plan, something always comes along to mess it up.
5. You need immediate results.
6. Thinking is not as important as doing, because when you're thinking, you're not really working.

We have many reasons for not preparing, such as thinking we can get away with not doing the work. And no doubt, some people can get away with it. Having the right connections can pay off. But for most of us, preparation is required. It means we must make sacrifices of our time to get to where we want to be. How easy it is to think that, if we've done something many times, we don't need to prepare. The ego says, "I know all there is to know." That's a setup for failure because even if you know the material, your audience changes, material constantly needs to be updated, something new always has to be learned.

Today I never go onstage without spending time preparing for my talk, regardless of whether it's my legal talk or my life story. I make sure I am comfortable with my material and know my audience before setting foot on the platform. Not to do so is disrespectful to my audience, because lack of preparation sends the message that my audience isn't important. Preparation keeps me fresh, current, in the moment, and interesting. Being prepared keeps me informed. For that reason, I prepare for everything, whether for a talk, an exam, or a client meeting. I wasn't always so vigilant, and I paid the price.

Each time I failed the New York Bar exam, it was because I wasn't fully prepared. Yes, I studied, but I wasn't prepared in the way I needed to be until I made passing the test a priority. On some level, I also thought what I learned in school was sufficient. I was wrong, and I failed. I wasn't prepared.

Today I know the value of preparation. And I don't take it for granted. Whether I'm getting ready for a talk I've given hundreds of times or doing a program for the first time, I put in the time to prepare. Preparation is the key to success in any venture. Taking the time to do what's needed is an esteemable act.

So how do you prepare? What are some questions you need to ask in getting ready for a task? Depending on your goal, your specific questions and concerns will be different, but the idea is to ask a lot of questions and get your answers in the beginning, not after the fact. Here are some questions to consider:

- What is expected of me?
- What's my purpose in performing the task?
- What's the ultimate outcome?
- When is the date of the event or the due date for the project?
- What is the thing I'm preparing for?
- Who is involved? Are there people I can talk to for information to help me prepare?
- If it's a presentation, who is my audience?
- How long will it take to do what I have to do?

- What resources do I need? Where can I get them?
- Are there limitations I should be aware of?

This week, you're invited to get prepared.

DAY 2

What event this week requires you to be prepared? Maybe it's a speech, a short presentation, a meeting, a class, a swim or track meet, or a ball game.

DAY 3

In order to succeed, what needs to be done? Make a list of all the actions you need to take to get ready for the success of this event or project. Don't forget to list the resources you need and an initial plan for where to find them.

DAY 4

Prioritize your activities and do something that takes you closer to the success you dream of. For example, do you need to go to the library to find resources? Do you need to arrange for child care?

DAY 5

Today take more preparatory action to move you closer to the success of this project. If you are worried, talk to a friend about your fears. Ask for feedback—you might hear some helpful ideas.

DAY 6

Are you feeling mentally prepared for the task? If so, focus on your physical preparation. Are you getting adequate rest and eating wisely? Don't let the basics of self-care become obstacles to your goals.

DAY 7

Once again, today you're invited to rest, recharge, regroup, and review your week. What observations can you make about your willingness to prepare for tasks? Was the preparation useful? Was one day more difficult than another? Why?

WEEK
51

Honor Your Healing Journey

Thought for the Week

Self-esteem comes from honoring
your healing journey.

Affirmations for the Week

I honor my healing journey.
This week, I will appreciate my own effort.

Esteemable Actions for the Week

DAY 1

My life is not perfect. I make a lot of mistakes. Sometimes I stumble
and fall. I am a work in progress. And when I remember that simple
fact, I am better for the experience.

It's easy to start on a path of change and get so busy doing what
we need to do that we forget to stop, breathe, and acknowledge the
effort we've already made. We forget to honor our own healing
journey.

There are times when I have to be reminded to do for myself
what I do for others. The other day, a friend caught me denigrating
the work I put into a project because it wasn't done perfectly. When
she asked how it was coming along, I said, "I can't seem to get it
down perfectly. It's horrible." I then spent ten minutes—which was

as long as she could tolerate my ranting—downplaying the work I had put into the project so far. She couldn't believe she was listening to me. "You could be one of your own clients," she said. And how right she was. I needed to be coached at that moment in time. And after our conversation, I called my coach.

Healing is hard work. It takes great effort to stay on a path that leads to purposeful self-discovery. It takes energy—persistent energy—to be an active participant in the creation of our lives. A healing path requires having the courage to shine a light or allow a light to shine on parts of ourselves that we'd rather keep private. It means having the courage to see the work that still needs to be done. Honoring our healing journey invites us to appreciate the effort that has been made. It's important to heal and to honor the work done.

What gets in the way of our honoring the amazing healing path we are on?

- We don't know how to honor ourselves. Often we've never done it before, and more likely, it's never been done to us. We learn how to honor ourselves by being honored.
- We don't know the right words to use to get our point across.
- We're afraid of what people will think if we appreciate our own effort. Women, particularly, have been taught that celebrating successes is not an appropriate thing to do. If women openly appreciate their accomplishments (other then those that relate to children), they are seen as pompous and self-congratulatory. I see this dynamic play out in my networking groups. The men are quite comfortable speaking about their businesses and what they have to offer. The women, on the other hand, are more reticent in speaking about what they do and how good they are.
- We're not good at honoring ourselves out loud. Sometimes we're willing, but because we're unskilled, it is easier not to speak at all.
- We feel guilty. Since others who are equally or more qualified haven't been recognized or don't recognize themselves, we feel we

shouldn't acknowledge ourselves. After I finally passed the New York Bar exam, I found it hard to relish my victory because of all the people who still hadn't passed or who hadn't been successful at something they attempted. In time, I got over that. No doubt, there were and continue to be people who miss their desired mark. But it's important for me in my quest to help others that I begin with honoring my own healing journey.

It's important to honor the journey we're on. It's crucial for our own well-being and mental health that we stop and appreciate every little step we take along this path called healing. So how do we do it?

- Make a commitment to yourself to honor what you do.
- Know that if you don't honor yourself, even if others do, it will be an empty win. No one can fill that hole inside you, except you.
- In your journal each night, write a gratitude list that includes some action you've taken that you are grateful for. Make this a daily activity.
- When someone gives you a compliment about an action you've taken, graciously say, "Thank you." Don't come up with a diatribe about what went wrong or why it wasn't perfect. Just say thank you.
- Say thank you to whomever helped you accomplish your goal. Saying thank you implies there's something to be grateful for.

This week, you're invited to practice honoring your healing journey.

DAY 2

Today think of something you did this week or in the last few weeks that moved you closer to healing in your life. Perhaps it was an action regarding a failed relationship or an action to create a relationship with your Higher Power. Speak about it aloud. Stand in the mirror, look at yourself, and repeat five times how proud you are of yourself for taking this action. You can use the following language if you like: "[Your name], what I appreciate about you is _____."

DAY 3

If you did yesterday's assignment as I asked, congratulations. If you didn't, what got in the way? And if you did any part of the assignment, I want you to say, "[Your name], I appreciate that you made an effort today by doing _____."

DAY 4

What gets in the way of you honoring your journey? What stands between you and appreciating the work you put into making something happen?

DAY 5

Each day in your journal, write a gratitude list that includes some action you've taken that you are grateful for. If you haven't started this activity already, begin today. Get into the habit of writing about what you've done well.

DAY 6

Today and all of this week, when anyone gives you a compliment, practice saying thank you. Nothing more, just thank you.

DAY 7

Finally, today is your day to rest, recharge, regroup, and review your week. What observations can you make about your willingness to honor your healing journey? Was it more of a challenge than you thought it would be? Why? What day seemed extra hard?

WEEK 52

Let Go of the Baggage

Thought for the Week

Self-esteem comes from seeing love as an action.

Affirmations for the Week

I feel my anger; then I work through it.

This week, I will not be held hostage
by my feelings.

Esteemable Actions for the Week

DAY 1

Have you ever gone shopping and then returned home with too many bags to carry? Have you ever chosen not to check your bags at the airport and instead lugged all your belongings onto the crowded plane? Did you feel heavy? Weighted down? No doubt, excess baggage weighs us down. We feel tired, sluggish, and often victimized because we have more to carry than other people. Yet the truth is, we all make choices about how much baggage we want to carry.

Anger and resentments are baggage, old stuff that weighs heavy on our heart and our mind. And in some cases, it's as damaging as our continually carrying too heavy a load on our small backs. Eventually, the back breaks from the load or from exhaustion. So it is with emotional baggage. Our emotional baggage comes when people disappoint us and we don't deal with it in the moment. It comes when we allow resentment to settle in, get comfortable, and take control of our lives. People let us down, whether or not they know it. They hurt us with their words, they disappoint us with their actions, and they don't follow through. When they hurt us, we feel justified in holding a grudge—forever.

Anger is a powerful intoxicant. We become so consumed with what has been done to us that we let anger define our attitude. What is it about anger that intoxicates so many of us? The "I am right" consciousness. This is the belief that we are right and they are wrong; therefore, we are justified in being mad. It took me years to let go of the anger I felt for my uncle.

I hadn't seen him for years. We hadn't shared a conversation in almost as many. Yet a feeling came over me that said it was time to clean up this relationship, let go of the past, and move into the future. So as I entered the new year, I decided that creating a greater connection with my family—all of them—was at the top of the list. Yes, my mother and I now enjoy a rich and special relationship. Yes, there are aunts and uncles I regularly keep in touch with. And sometimes I call my sister. But there was that one member of my family from whom I was estranged. And something inside me called out to change that relationship. I got the message loud and clear that this is my year to make it happen.

Too often our efforts at healing come when someone is gravely ill or about to die. I've always wondered, why do we wait until it's too late to do what our heart yearns to do? Why do we wait to the point of saying, "I wish I would have . . ." when indeed we could have?

As humans, we get tough and purport to be strong, yet our innards are so fragile. Our heart breaks easily and our feelings get hurt almost at the blink of an eye or the slip of a tongue. There may be valid reasons to be angry, but for a lifetime? That seems an awfully long time to allow someone to live rent-free in your brain. For years my uncle had lived rent-free in my brain. I allowed him to. No, I didn't think of him every day or even every month. But when something triggered a thought of him, there was always an emotional eruption.

As I approached this new year, I decided I needed and wanted to make peace with my uncle. He was my family. My reasons are varied: he's getting old, I'm getting older, I no longer wanted to live with that knot in my gut, I need to tend to unfinished business, I want to walk even more like I talk, family is important, and I just didn't want to wake up one morning after his death saying, "I wish I would have done it differently." In the real world, there is the family we are born into and the family we create. There will be struggles to overcome within each family system. It took me years to realize that the issues in my family of origin are often re-created in my family of choice, and vice versa—that's human nature. People aren't really very different. I am, and have always been, the common denominator in every family I've been a part of.

This week, you're invited to revisit the labels you've attached to people.

DAY 2

Today you're invited to identify a preconceived idea or set of ideas you hold about a particular person you're angry with. Maybe it's a family member, maybe it's a friend, maybe it's someone you were intimate with. Whoever it is, think of the label you've attached to that person. Write about it today.

DAY 3

Today examine why you've held on to the label you attached to the person you mentioned in day 2. What is it about him or her or the situation that makes you want to hold on tightly? What's the payoff? What benefit are you getting from being angry at that person for weeks, months, or years?

DAY 4

What would it take to change your mind about the person mentioned in day 2? Is there something they need to do to make you feel better? What if you never get what you need? Be mindful that if your level of comfort depends on someone else changing who they are, you may be waiting for a long time. So suppose they aren't going to change, or they are willing to change but are not willing to make the first move. What are you willing to do for your peace of mind and emotional comfort?

DAY 5

Today think about someone who may have a long-term grudge against you. Of course, some people don't like us and we have no idea they feel that way because they've never told us. There are also times when, no matter what we do, we can never make things right. But I suspect you can recall a person whom you are no longer connected to, perhaps someone who was a friend. And perhaps if you were to make the first move, your deed would set in motion the divine law of healing.

DAY 6

Today is the day to practice letting go of your resentments. It's not a day when you just give lip service to letting go, but a day when you really hunker down and do the work necessary for a real healing to take place. Here are some things to keep in mind:

- Letting go of anger is a choice you make.
- Holding on to anger is easy. It takes work to move through a conflict and see another person's side, more than most of us want to put out.
- Anger makes you feel in control. When you're mad at someone, you think you are in control of the relationship, but actually it is

the other person who is really in command of your heart, mind, and soul.

- While your feelings may be valid, consider picking your battles carefully. Is it worth living with anger for your lifetime and the lifetime of your children? Your anger doesn't just live inside of you, it lives in everyone you come in contact with. You spread it wherever you go, whether consciously or unconsciously.

- Know that sometimes people who encourage you to hold on to anger have an investment in seeing you mad.

- Feeling your feelings is one thing; getting stuck in them is another.

- Finally, do you often expect more of others than you do of yourself? How often do you expect others to do what you're unwilling to do? Have you ever made a mistake, done something outrageously stupid, or disappointed yourself? Has anything silly, embarrassing, or inflammatory ever come out of your mouth and you wish you hadn't said it? Of course. Did you stop talking to yourself for days, weeks, months, or even years because you made such a blunder? Of course not. Yet how often have you been disappointed or hurt by someone and you held a grudge for days, weeks, months, or years? Why do you expect people to be perfect, yet demand your right to be a human being who makes mistakes?

DAY 7

Finally, today is your day to rest, recharge, regroup, and review your week. What observations can you make about your willingness to see love as an action? Was it more of a challenge than you thought it would be? Why? What day seemed extra hard?

About the Author

A former practicing lawyer, Francine Ward is now a highly sought-after executive coach, life coach, and motivational speaker. In addition to this book, she is the author of *Esteemable Acts: 10 Actions for Building Real Self-Esteem*.

Based on the concepts that led to her remarkable recovery from addiction, alcoholism, a sordid past, and low self-esteem, Ward's compelling message of walking through fear as a way to build self-esteem—one baby step at a time—is a courageous new path to freedom. Her powerful message: Anything is possible if you are willing to do the work—no matter where you come from. And you don't have to hurt others to get there.

A 1989 graduate of Georgetown University Law Center, she was admitted to the New York State Bar. She is a member of the American Bar Association's Intellectual Property Law Section, the National Speakers Association, the American Society for Training and Development, and the International Coach Federation. She is also an active Rotarian.

For more information about inviting Ward to speak at your next event or purchasing her products or coaching services, please feel free to browse her Web site at www.esteemableacts.com or call 1-866-ESTEEMABLE.